A CHURCH
FOR ALL
AGES

A practical approach
to all age worship

Peter Graystone and Eileen Turner

Scripture Union
130 City Road London EC1V 2NJ

© Peter Graystone and Eileen Turner 1993

First published 1993
Reprinted 1994, 1996

ISBN 0 86201 859 5

British Library Cataloguing-in-Publication Data.
A catalogue record for this book is available from the British Library.

Cover design by Julian Smith.
Book design by Tony Cantale Graphics
Phototypeset by Intype, London.

Printed and bound in Great Britain by Cox & Wyman Ltd, Reading, Berkshire.

CONTENTS

Part One – ADVICE

Part Two – RESOURCES

Part One
ADVICE

This book is dedicated to the leaders and congregations of St Andrews Church, Wakefield, and Emmanuel Church, South Croydon, who started us thinking about all-age worship and allowed us to try out much of what is in this book.

1
TOO GOOD TO RESIST?

All-age worship is like jam. Even if we rarely sample it, we can't help having ideas about what it is. It comes in all shapes and sizes, flavours and consistencies. Sometimes it is named strawberry jam or plum jam; but it can also be redcurrant jelly or even orange marmalade. And what about chocolate spread and peanut butter! Perhaps the inclusive term *preserve* would be a more appropriate comparison. Many understand the concept without using the word. Several years ago British lovers of ginger marmalade were startled to discover it had been reclassified as ginger preserve because it did not fit the official EC definition of marmalade. Such a pedantic attitude might irritate us, but it can be helpful to define something by what it is not. All-age worship is *not* children's worship or a family service or junior church, though it has some features in common with these. All-age worship is about a cross-section of people worshipping God together. Like jam, which is thick, sweet and sticky, some people avoid it on health grounds or prefer it spread very thinly. Preserve, however, sounds a bit more sophisticated, encompasses the savoury as well as the sweet, and implies not just luxury but survival!

All-age through the ages

As liturgy developed in the Western world it was usually an adult preserve. Neville Clarke described a child in church as 'an unconnected pendant, awkward, ill-fitting, somehow painfully to be related to the finished product set before him' (*Worship and the Child*, Joint Liturgical Group, 1975). The

Sunday School movement, which began in the late eighteenth century, has probably been the greatest single influence on the position of children in the church. Before the Industrial Revolution any religious instruction took place within the family; but when home and workplace separated, Sunday Schools were started to meet the general educational needs of deprived children. They continued long after educational opportunities improved, becoming an integral part of all major denominations and influencing huge numbers of the nation's children. Unfortunately the very success of Sunday Schools obscured their drawbacks. Few people questioned the suitability of the school model, or the danger of their increasing autonomy.

After the Second World War new sociological factors came into play. The standard of living rose and children found more to interest them, including television which appeared in most homes. Car ownership began to transform the traditional family Sunday. Whereas in the 1930s and '40s two-thirds of the nation's children had been involved, and in the '50s still half, during the next two decades attendances dropped rapidly. Children opted out at all ages but particularly around the age of eleven. Because Sunday Schools relied on children being *sent*, usually during the afternoon, this was not surprising, for the majority of parents had been given the message, implicitly if not explicitly, that adults do not go to church. However good the teaching, Sunday Schools could only provide children's worship. Their members had little concept of 'church', indeed some may have rarely entered the church building, and thus had no grounding for future adult membership.

The numbers crisis forced churches to think very seriously. In an attempt to bring Sunday School and church closer together many children's groups moved from afternoon to morning. Occasional 'family services', often including uniformed organisations, had long been the custom in some areas but now concepts like 'children's church', 'junior church' and 'family church' began to emerge. A completely new approach to Christian education within the context of adult worship had been pioneered by 'Bert' Hamilton, a Congregationalist. In the 1930s he had experimented with the first scheme for churches splitting into age groups for thematic learning after worshipping together; and also with 'church friends', a link between children and Christian adults.

Though his ideas were sometimes rejected by Sunday School enthusiasts, they slowly had their influence. By 1950, half the Congregational (later United Reformed) churches had adopted his system and the next two decades brought experimentation in all denominations. There was no single pattern; children's activities might parallel the morning service, overlap it, or be totally integrated with it. Sunday Schools had always been more open to new ideas than the rest of the church and during this period there was a surge of excellent teaching material. However the emphasis was still more on learning than on worship, and learning took place in a teacher/pupil format, rather than a more experiential one. Where children spent the whole time in their own departments they were almost as separate as in the old system.

In the Anglican church the issue was complicated by the Parish Communion movement which also dates back to the 1930s. Every age-group was encouraged to attend one main service and this was a eucharist, 'the Lord's service for the Lord's people on the Lord's day'. At first this had little impact on the evangelical wing of the church, but during the 1970s eucharistic worship become more central both to Anglicans and other denominations, such as the church of Scotland. Different patterns emerged, not dissimilar to those described above, though the most common was for children to join the adult congregation part-way through the service.

In some locations the eucharist was recognised as being too exclusive, particularly in inner cities and other areas where not every member of a family was a regular worshipper. Here it was sometimes supplemented by an additional act of worship, often at an earlier time. These 'family services' were particularly popular in large churches and those serving developing areas. Though excellent at drawing in parents and children, they have sometimes been criticised for over-emphasising the 'family' ethos and having a rather simplistic approach. The anticipated transfer from one congregation to another happened less than was hoped, and often the two types of service remained in parallel, hindering rather than helping the integration of the whole church.

The last few decades have seen the rapid growth of new churches with their worship inviting an open and spontaneous use of all the gifts the Holy Spirit gives. This has encouraged exciting experiment in many other denominations. With the need to establish new patterns of adult spirituality high on the agenda in the early years, it is only recently that serious consideration has been given to the special requirements of bringing adults and children together. There is a growing impetus from this new wing of the church to make the main service of every week an intergenerational one on a Sunday morning, with supplementary children's groups and adult Bible study on a weekday evening. While some still feel that adults and children fit uncomfortably together in this kind of 'Spirit-led' worship, it is clear that the format is going to become increasingly popular and will also have an impact on churches of other traditions.

Traditional models – helpful or confusing?

Though at one level the Sunday School movement was hugely successful, there is little to show for it today and many elderly teachers in dwindling congregations must wonder whether all their effort and devotion was in vain. The 'school' model evolved from historical circumstances, not for theological reasons, and pinned too much hope on the technique of the classroom. In any case, many teachers were untrained and inexperienced and, in the early days, much teaching material was poor. Some teaching was excellent, of course, as successful results in Bible 'exams' demonstrated, though we might question the lasting benefit of such knowledge. Two-thirds of today's church members say they took significant steps towards faith as children, but this is a relatively small proportion of the original attenders. Those who look back nostalgically on Sunday School days talk mostly of the character of the teacher or the annual outing. However good the Sunday School experience, it was often more about belonging to a 'club' than being part of the whole church; gaining head knowledge rather than knowing God.

If all-age worship is not Sunday 'School', neither is it just 'family' worship. Of course, 'family' (not in the sense of blood relationship, but in the sense of the community of an extended household) is a biblical image. In Galatians 6:10 Paul urges us to 'do good to those who belong to our family in the faith': in Ephesians 3:15 he prays to the Father 'from whom every family in heaven and earth receives its true name.' Of all the models of church, family is one of the most useful, but it is still only one among many and if over-emphasised can create problems. In the 1970s liturgists sometimes talked as if the church could move toward the biblical concept of family by using the Christian family as a pattern – an unhelpful idea since it was not clear what was meant by either. It was used successfully to support the idea of one service for all ages and did help bring children into the centre of the church community, but already concern was being expressing about the 'loading' of the word 'family'.

Recently the idea of the family has been subject to searching theological enquiry. Many criticise the church for an over-emphasis, almost a glorifying, of the nuclear family. It is all too easy to let a romantic mixture of Old Testament, Victorian patriarchalism, and post-war middle-class idealism become a model for the church. This can make children too central, distort the role of women, overload us with sentimentality and blind us to the true facts of life. In fact the New Testament teaching about family can be quite disturbing. In Matthew 10:34–37 Jesus uses strong words, warning that the Gospel may sometimes cause division in families and suggesting that our love for him must far exceed our love of family members. His attitude to his own human family is ambiguous. Whilst he obviously made their welfare a high priority, he sometimes seems to take the relationships quite lightly (John 19:26–27, Matthew 12:46–50). The latter passage tells us that Jesus used a visit from his mother and brothers as an opportunity to hint that the human family is meant as a 'taster' of something even better. Presumably his words, 'Who is my mother? Who are my brothers?' were said with gentle humour to preface his interesting comment about his disciples, 'Look! here are my mother and my brothers! Whoever does what my Father in heaven wants him to do is my brother, my sister, and my mother.' This same idea is echoed in Mark 10:29–30 where Jesus promises even richer relationships within God's kingdom for those who give up much for him. Thus the New Testament thrust is about putting God first and seeing the family of origin as a means to this rather than an end in itself.

The title 'family service' is widely used on occasions when adults, teenagers and children are present. It is emphasised that, whilst families provide a section of the clientele, the event is for the whole church 'family'. The hope is that those with unhappy family experiences might even find healing as the word 'family' takes on new meaning. However, some may wish to play down the use of the word in this context.

We live in a society where ideas about family are in flux, where household patterns vary enormously, and where half the population, for one reason or other, is single. Though we continue to emphasise some good things about the traditional nuclear family, we also want the church to be accessible to those whose lifestyle is different. As with sexist or racist language, it can be counter-productive to keep using a word once it has taken on a certain flavour. Alternative models are the 'pilgrim people', which suggests going on a journey together and 'community'. Both of these suggest the church as a loose, flexible system in which we come and go, experience a whole range of healthy relationships, finding our home life is enriched whilst at the same time being protected from its excesses. The modelling process is thus reversed: the church will be providing a blue-print for personal relationships rather than describing itself in the language of inadequate human systems. The worship of such a community might be better described as all-age rather than 'family', though judging by the reluctance of the title 'Sunday School' to lie down and die, this will certainly not happen overnight!

All-age worship is good for children

While it was often said that Sunday Schools were building the 'church of tomorrow', we now hear frequently that children are already part of the church; that they have a present role not just a probationary one; that they should be included in the church's worship in their own right. The way things were done in the past may sometimes have given them the idea that worship and learning were quite separate. We are now more likely to say that, though worship is a unique activity, many other experiences are associated with it and taken up into it. Along with the home, it is the main context for Christian growth, the place where faith is primarily passed on, and through which we acquire Christian language. Taking children seriously does pose many questions about worship patterns, but the issue is not about finding a 'lowest common denominator'. Explaining Hamilton's vision in the 1940s, Philip Cliff describes worship as bringing 'a sense of transcendence, the sense of the numinous' and goes on to say that 'children might not understand this at a cognitive level, but affectively they would be aware and would experience that which later they would come to attempt to understand intellectually' (*The Rise and Development of the Sunday School Movement in England*, National Christian Educational Council, 1986).

Almost everywhere nowadays the Sunday morning service is the main event at which all church members can in theory meet together. The tendency is towards more informality, though churches vary enormously and even where the congregation is open to the freedom of allowing the Spirit to shape the pattern of worship, a sort of unwritten liturgy often develops. Our debate is not about whether this or that service best teaches children about worship, but about whether they are seen to be a genuine part of whatever is the norm for each particular congregation. Whether structured or not, any service can be enriched by the presence of children and, as Colin Buchanan put it over twenty years ago, they might 'do us a good turn by helping us unfreeze the liturgy'. He described communion as 'an activity which is not avowedly or implicitly childish, but is not exclusive of children' and saw 'the combination of singing, word, spectacle and action as well adapted psychologically to involving children's attention and interest' (*Nurturing Children in Communion*, Grove Booklets on Ministry and Worship No.9, 1972).

There are few nowadays who would say that because neither traditional nor charismatic worship are primarily designed for children all attempts to integrate them are counter-productive. Indeed, if anything in a service is totally unsuitable for children perhaps we should ask whether it is really suitable for all adults. If the presence of children spoils something precious to us, we might gain interesting insights about ourselves by asking what it is that is so important. Neville Clark, in *Worship and the Child*, talks of each Christian community needing 'one liturgy' for all its people. This does not assume that the age-groups spend every moment together, for we cannot deny that some dimensions of worship are more appropriately explored in one's own peer group. But this way of thinking does set boundaries and guards against children limiting their experience to the sort of worship they have in their own group. Everyone is entitled to their preferences, but that brings an implicit responsibility to respect the preferences of others, and a challenge to explore ways other than our own. It is good for children and newcomers to learn to value the traditions of the church, but other adults may need to sacrifice some things which are dear. Learning to accept each others' cultural preferences is important in our growth together toward Christian maturity, and worshipping alongside children is a relatively painless way of having the 'corners knocked off'.

All-age worship is good for teenagers

Many churches worry about their ministry to young people, and the drop-out rate in the teenage years is even more disappointing now fewer children are attending in the first place. Newer styles of children's ministry may have resulted in them becoming more integrated in the church, but few have been recruited from non-Christian backgrounds. In addition, the drop in child attendance during the 1980s was greater than the drop in adult attendance, though this is partly explained by demographic factors. Even if we include Christian schools, the church is now in contact with only 14% of the nation's children. These rather confusing statistics say two things to us. First that we must again take children's evangelism seriously, though it is usually recognised that the regular weekly service is not now the most appropriate occasion for this. Second, though very few teenagers attend church, those who do are probably from Christian families or have already faced the challenge of being in a minority in their peer group.

Some might say the teenage group gains least benefit from all-age worship. 'The timing is all wrong because Sunday morning is for bed or homework! The music is all wrong for teenagers are most unappreciative of what adults think are trendy modern songs. The clientele is all wrong, particularly for those who have parents around'. This stage is particularly hard for young people as they seek, consciously or unconsciously, an expression of faith which is all their own. It would be odd if this did not include some criticism of what they observe or have grown up in. Teenagers need their own group identity, probably more than any other section of the church, and ideally each congregation will take seriously the need adequately to resource special youth ministries. Where low numbers or finances make this difficult it is sometimes possible for several churches to tackle it together.

This is not to say, however, that there is no place for teenagers in all-age worship. Sometimes this will be the one opportunity for them to meet those younger and older than themselves on an equal footing. When they leave a group, having reached the top of the age range or fallen out with their best friend, church-going may well continue if it has been established as a regular pattern. Teenagers of the past stayed around when they had a role in a choir or helping with a creche or Sunday School class. Today, an 'adult' job such as working the PA system or as a member of the music group, gives them a purpose and can provide stability in their times of questioning. We should not be surprised if one minute they are on a spiritual 'high', the next totally bored with church. Though we may find it hard, it is best to avoid criticism if their attendance is erratic and watch our language when they reappear after an absence. As adults we have to keep reminding ourselves of the teenager's need to be 'there but not there'; to allow them to congregate in a corner and within limits to turn 'a blind eye'. Experience shows that young adults who have been nurtured in an all-age atmosphere often retain good feelings about the church. Many still talk as if they belong years after drifting away. Presumably they will be receptive if and when they return at some time in the future.

All-age worship is good for all ages

A look at the teenage culture reminds us how polarised Western society has become. Each of us lives in several subcultures, and different age-groups rarely have the opportunity to mix on a regular basis. Children and elderly people watch their own TV programmes and attend their own clubs. Often their paths never cross and they are mistrustful of each other. Single people often find it hard to find a way into a society that is geared to couples. Some of us wear different 'masks' at work and home and church and with our friends. Some professions rarely mix socially with those from other walks of life. Rather than doing the same and becoming a 'culture' all of its own, the church could take a lead and proclaim more strongly its message about breaking down barriers.

Galatians 3:28 tells us of the miracle of very disparate groups coming together: 'There is no difference between Jews and Gentiles, between slaves and free men, between men and women; you are all one in union with Christ Jesus.' The growing New Testament church struggled painfully to work out this truth and the problems raised were both theological and practical. The argument in Acts 15, about whether or not new Christians should conform to Judaism, helps us see that differences of opinion are to be expected and are quite normal. In a similar way the church sometimes struggles with what it believes about the position of children. We have moved far from the Old Testament model of family as the main place of nurture, with the child's standing before God dependent on the attitude of parents, and it is hard to grasp how great is this change. Our modern view, that children are to be thought of as individuals, is consistent with Jesus' attitude. He lived in a society which thought little of them, yet clearly enjoyed their company and was angry when the disciples dismissed them (Mark 10:13–16). To settle arguments about who was the most important, he used children as examples of what adults should be like in order to enter God's kingdom (Matthew 18:1–4). Even when they made a noise in the Temple he did not mind, again treating them as 'insiders', as people with something to say (Matthew 21:15–16). This is consistent, too, with modern psychology which reinforces the need for children to develop a positive self-image and be accepted for themselves in the community.

Another biblical picture shows us vividly how different age groups might relate together in the church. 1 Corinthians 12:12–27 describes a 'body', each part having a different role, some more prominent than others, yet totally inter-dependent. The age-groups will never be evenly balanced: at one stage a church may be dominated by one group, a decade later by another. Nevertheless a church which sees its inter-generational life as important will be less likely to miss out a whole age-group. Smaller churches, which struggle to maintain children's ministry, will find this particularly significant. In practice this unity can be a first step to the other unities we long for. A church which has learned tolerance and patience through handling the integration of different age groups will find minority groups, such as the disabled or ethnic minorities, easier to absorb and will perhaps approach dialogue with other denominations and other faiths with more confidence.

All-age worship is good for 'grown ups'

Another gain for adults is the relatively easy access to the hidden parts of our personalities. Each of us has a 'child' inside, but the need to preserve dignity and efficiency, to keep going in the 'rat race' of life, means we often neglect that vulnerable yet spontaneous and creative part of us. Being a parent provides some opportunities for play, but does not guarantee that this part of our personality will continue to be developed sufficiently. The business executive might 'play hard' in the sense of competitive sports, yet rarely have the opportunity to enjoy the absurd. In the Western world Christian faith is often more a matter of the head than the heart, and all-age activities can help change that balance. Adults worshipping alongside children find it easier to allow this 'child' out. This isn't just about 'action choruses and quizzes', though many an adult is grateful for the permission to join in with these. It is about nurturing the ingenuous, expectant bits of us; about using skills we have neglected; about enjoying the sensual in our communication with God. Children can teach us to trust; to relax and be our true selves; to bring out the best in each other.

All-age worship is good for newcomers

Though all-age worship is certainly not simplistic, the fact that children's needs are taken into account inevitably makes the whole church experience easier for newcomers. The success of 'family services' taught us that unchurched adults cope better with an informal atmosphere and often welcome an excuse to accompany children. Whilst about half the parents of adolescents and young adults have had some grounding in the faith, many young families are now headed by the second generation of non-Sunday-School parents. Thus people in church for the first time, whether or not accompanied by children, may have no preconceived ideas about what *should* happen and no previous Christian teaching. Although there is a certain amount of hostility toward the Christian religion among those who have given up on it, there is little evidence of hostility toward God. Many talk as if they have drifted away from the faith rather than deliberately rejected it. Most of the population of Britain still professes to believe in God and many claim their religion is important to them. Christians disagree about whether this 'folk religion' is a help or a hindrance to the spread of the Gospel, but when such people come to church we can be aware of how they might be thinking about God.

One good thing about the Sunday Schools of the past was

that, in spite of the huge cultural gap between the church and the working class, they succeeded in bringing the Gospel into that culture. During the last few decades family services have come the nearest to answering that need. Their weakness, however, has been a failure to bring new adults into the full life of the church. In the nurture of new members, worship together can be more important than education, particularly for the less articulate. The Anglican report *Patterns for Worship* discusses the need for services to reflect local culture in the inner city, something which cannot come solely from a group of experts. Hopefully it will evolve from an environment which encourages forms of public worship which are genuinely appropriate at a local level, but still recognisably at one with the character of the mainstream worship of the denomination or grouping to which the church belongs. The need to provide a valid worship experience for newcomers and for those who are mature in the faith guards against the content becoming simplistic, yet preserves the vitality of family-service-type worship.

So what is all-age worship?

So all-age worship is a genuine intergenerational activity: young and old in age and young and old in the faith worshipping together, perhaps not spending every minute of every service together but nevertheless knowing they are part of each other throughout. All-age worship is a good thing for pragmatic, educational, sociological, theological and psychological reasons. Pragmatic because the church is not too healthy; educational because old learning models are being questioned; sociological because our society has become so polarised; theological because the Bible tells of a church without barriers; psychological because we all need to belong before we can find ourselves.

And all age-worship is like jam! It is about preserving what is good from the past; though never preserving something for the sake of it. It is not the 'preserve' of children or families but belongs to everyone. On the one hand 'jam' conjures up a tricky situation in which we need to keep our wits about us; on the other hand 'jammy' reminds us of something easy and pleasant! All-age worship can be both these because it embraces the whole range of human experience.

2
A FORMAT THAT FITS

'But Daddy, we're on holiday, surely we don't have to go to church!' Many of us, after five minutes visiting a different church, wish we had listened to that warning! Of course the 'little darlings' would normally be beautifully behaved, but the strange building, the funny hymns, the odd smells and staring faces, the effect of yesterday's sun and sand, all combine to make a Sunday morning nightmare! Like choosing suitable restaurants, parents eventually get an instinct about where to find a genuine welcome, but there is rarely much choice even in highly populated areas, and it helps to be in an ecumenical frame of mind. Our dream is for any combination of people – single, married, family or other group – to be able to walk into any place of worship on any Sunday and find the opportunity for each individual to worship God appropriately. Unfortunately the only congregation we can change is our own, and even that can seem impossible!

Permutations and problems

This chapter is about structures, but even a system which runs like a well-oiled machine can still leave people feeling uncomfortable. The newcomer, feeling confused about when to sit or stand and what to do with a pile of books, is oblivious of the meticulous planning. The parent, embarrassed when a child refuses to leave the service after fifteen minutes, fails to appreciate the educational arguments for learning in peer groups. The couple whose children have left home, irritated by toddlers, forget the theology of all-age worship. We cannot totally eliminate these feelings, but we can anticipate them and understand that even people who have paid lip service to a plan might not like it quite so much in practice! No system can please everyone, and we should not expect total conformity, encouraging the kind of tolerance which allows people to 'break the rules' when they need to.

The all-age ethos is not about forcing everyone in every church on every Sunday to spend every minute together. The right format depends on recent history; the culture of the neighbourhood; the size of congregation; the resources of buildings, equipment and leadership; the overall teaching and worship plan. It is affected by the emphasis on expository preaching, formal liturgy, the sacraments or the use of spiritual gifts. What was right for a church ten years ago may not be best for now. It is exciting to see all-age worship ideas being worked out in a multitude of ways in the practice of different denominations and church cultures.

The permutations are endless. Children may worship with adults all the time, at the beginning or at the end, and the pattern might vary week by week. There are pros and cons to all plans. If adults and children are always together a short sermon can reach them simultaneously at different levels, but they will miss out on the learning which is best done in small peer groups; the former on Bible teaching and prayers which require a long attention span, the latter on the fun and more concrete applications involving craft and drama and informal chat. Where children only attend part of the service, we may get the best or the worst of all worlds. At best, age groups are separated for activities that work most effectively that way and the overlap is well planned and provides links. At worst, teaching time is too brief to get anything done; no one connects the various sections of the service; the children slip in or out without anyone noticing and muddle through without a hymn book or whatever else they need.

Timing is always hard and we must not mind when a system breaks down, as in one church where communion had completely finished before the children arrived, so they started all over again! However, if children are always experiencing only one small section of the service we must consider what impression this gives. If they consistently leave after the first fifteen minutes it may be that their only experience of corporate church life is of adults on their knees asking for forgiveness! Perhaps they think we never get it! For some, adult worship consists solely of the administration of communion, or incomprehensible and noisy songs of praise. In one church, until someone realised how absurd it was, they only experienced the notices and half a hymn! Those who never sit through a whole service may miss the opportunity to learn discipline in worship, including such things as handling a book or concentrating on an overhead projector screen, and find it hard to cope with later. If there are some aspects of church life which children never experience, perhaps a Lord's supper which always takes place in the evening, it might be worth checking whether this is church policy or is just accidental.

Whatever the system there must be flexibility within it: if little children usually stay in there should also be some facility to take the restless ones out; if children usually go out a suitable part of the room could be set aside for those who do not conform. Whatever plan is chosen, we can also experiment with new ideas from time to time: short-term learning in small groups for adults; an informal service including a communion-lunch, sometimes known as a 'love-feast' or 'agape'; evening all-age worship after a 'bring-and-share' tea; worship during an outing or church weekend. Indeed, in traditional churches where there is opposition to change, such times are ideal for gently feeding in new ideas! Good communication is particularly essential when changes are proposed and these demand a huge time investment and the total commitment of the team which leads teaching and worship. It is in every way more satisfactory for the shared life of the church if alterations to the worship structure are 'owned' by the whole congregation and not just perceived as being imposed by the minister or church committee.

It is wonderful when the church's learning scheme is also owned by the whole congregation. Sometimes the only clue adults get about what the children do in their peer groups is when they arrive home clutching their artwork; and it probably never crosses the children's minds what the adults might have studied and prayed about. How satisfactorily it would unite a church if, on any one Sunday, each group studied the same theme, approaching the same or related Bible passages from slightly different angles and discussing their practical application in the most appropriate way for their age! More and more churches are trying to put an integrated learning scheme in place and this has enormous advantages for those who lead any part of the service when all ages are together, however short or long. When this time is very limited it can be used more effectively, and in churches which vary the pattern almost every Sunday more continuity is possible. And who knows what conversations develop over lunch as different generations discover that their minds have been occupied with the same issues! Scripture Union's *SALT programme* is such a scheme. Its four-year cycle of teaching and worship not only provides resources for occasions when all ages are together, but also offers peer-group activities for Bible study, life application, praise and prayer in five age-bands, ranging from three years to adult. There are also resources produced by various denominations and church groups, providing expertise and imagination, on top of which there is still room for spontaneity and the individual touch.

Which plan is best?

Each congregation has to work out the best scheme for its own peculiar set of circumstances. Remember, though, that these circumstances change and it is worth having a re-think every few years! When one church questioned why it held a girls' Bible class at 3pm it was discovered that it had originally been the only time girls 'in service' were free – probably half a century out of date! Here are eight patterns which are all quite common:

A. **Children and adults never worship together, but follow the same themes at the same time at their own level**. It would be stretching the imagination to call this all-age worship, but at least there is a discernible link and parents and children who are motivated can compare notes later. Under this system children's leaders can become very isolated.

B. **Children and adults spend the first twenty minutes together, then split into peer groups**. This gives the opportunity to enjoy worship while people are still awake and keen, and to introduce the theme while everyone is together. It is perhaps one of the easier plans for newcomers, especially families, since it allows all to spend some time worshipping together before being segregated. However, if the first part is led by someone reluctant to commit themselves to the all-age ethos, it can feel very forced. Children's leaders do not lose contact with the adult congregation.

C. **Children and adults start separately, then join for worship or communion**. Many in formal churches have found this a fairly gentle first step into all-age worship. Children's leaders can set up their rooms with interesting opening activities and can greet children individually. Those who come without parents will find this easier than the model above, particularly on the first occasion. The children have a chance to display what has been done in age-groups and perhaps to lead a worship item they have preapred without waiting until the next week. Also they can share at some level in the sacramental life of the church, though it can seem odd only to experience the end of a communion service and it is worth giving thought as to how to make it a climax rather than an anti-climax. The entry of children's groups can be difficult to organise unless there is a proper break. Sometimes there is a rush of excited energy as children re-enter, and though a sensitive leader can use this creatively, there are times when it will feel disruptive.

D. **One Sunday per month all ages worship together, and for the rest are apart for the whole service**. Because this introduces all-age worship in such a way that everyone knows exactly what the boundaries are, it feels safe in many churches. It certainly gives a high profile to the intergenerational life of a church. However, sometimes the monthly service together develops such a different style that non-regulars will hardly believe it is happening in the same church! There is also the danger that enthusiastic leaders may tend toward a children-orientated performance rather than all-age worship. This system does give children's leaders a week off, though it has also been known for other members of the congregation who are resistant to change to take a week off as well!

E. **A combination of (D) with either (B) or (C)**. This gives lots of opportunities to try out all-age ideas, without giving the impression that there is just one new way to do things. It is very hard to sustain unless there is an integrated learning scheme. It can also be slightly confusing until the pattern is well established, and even then is rather a problem for non-regulars. Any model where one group 'comes in' or 'goes out' can interrupt the flow and give the impression that one part of the service is more valuable, but some churches successfully include children both at the beginning and the end! Any system can be made to work so long as it seems right for those particular circumstances and everyone is committed to it.

F. **An all-age service, followed by an adult service, every week**. This pattern enables a church which is totally committed to all-age worship to keep within its fellowship those who simply cannot cope with this. It also caters for 'fringe' church-goers who can escape after the accessible all-age part. During the course of a Sunday morning, everyone's needs can potentially be met, though some helpers are required to organise games or other children's activities while the adults are having their teaching. Occasionally children can fall foul of such a system: attending only the second because of parental choice, or even finding themselves involved in both, as all-age participant at one and choir member at the other! The system works well while a good number of people attend both services, but one result of success may be that they start to split into two separate congregations. It is important to be aware if this is happening and make a definite choice either to work at sustaining the links (refreshments between services; more continuity between the two parts; worship and social events at other times) or to encourage the idea of separate development in the same way that one might nurture the separate development of a church plant. Robert Warren describes how, after an initial reluctance, the decision was taken in a north of England church to go for separate 'congregations', each with its own leadership, pastoral and social networks (*In the Crucible*, Highland Books, 1989). This experience, which turned out to be very freeing, is at the moment the exception rather than the rule, but it illustrates how God's plan for a church might not be the most obvious one!

G. **An all-age service every Sunday with children and adults together for the whole time; supplemented by adult-level teaching and worship on a week night and children's midweek groups for teaching and recreation**. The church which adopts this system is really making a statement about the importance of all-age worship! All ages are seen as equally welcome in church, though it is worth checking out from time to time that everyone does feel included.

Such a format requires a high time commitment and motivation level by adults, particularly the leaders. It can be difficult to avoid the 'should's and 'ought's about midweek meetings, which may be attended by those very people who might be better at home with their families or developing friendships with unchurched neighbours in the community!

H. **Occasional all-age days of combined learning, recreation, creativity and worship on Saturdays or bank holidays, in combination with any of the above.** Any church could fall into this category by taking the risk of arranging one such event! There is nothing like it for getting to know each other and it gives ample opportunity to try out ideas which still seem a little unusual for Sundays in church. Even if some mistakes are made, such a day is likely to be a success because everyone is feeling relaxed. However, it will not happen without considerable organisation.

Looking after leaders

Those in leadership roles need to be cared for themselves. Because the work of children's leaders is often taken for granted, it is especially necessary to build in support systems for them. Enthusiasm, and the difficulty of finding replacements, leads many to continue long after they should be taking a different role or having a break. In churches where it is known that becoming involved with children's work is not a 'life sentence', it will be easier to recruit new leadership. It can be very creative for a team to include both men and women, young and not-so-young, parents and singles, 'professional' teachers and those who are not; also to supplement the regular leadership with occasional help from an elderly or heavily committed church member who would otherwise have no chance to work with children. A large church might be able to appoint someone to head the team, with sole responsibility for training and pastoral care; but in a small congregation, with only one or two people involved, this need is just as great. It is important to ensure that children's leaders have the opportunity for their own input or, if the team is large enough, are able to take a few weeks off occasionally. If the church has a system for discerning who serves in which 'jobs', then the task of deployment, including that of discouraging over-enthusiastic volunteers, is more manageable.

Now the days of the totally autonomous Sunday School department are gone, the role of liaising between minister(s), children's leaders and parents is a crucial one. Much all-age worship fails to turn out as planned because no-one knows who is meant to do what! There is a continual need to double-check, especially when something new is happening, and the link person, who has to combine infinite tact with a 'thick skin', will inevitably feel a terrible nuisance! Though it can sometimes be a shock for the church, one real advantage of all-age worship is that children and their leaders have a higher profile. Most of the worship models listed above provide ideal opportunities for new people to try out their gifts in a small way in an all-age setting. It is important to remember that leading worship and speaking require different skills, and though many people develop both some will be happier doing one or the other both in church and with separate age-groups.

Buildings and babies

The illegibility of some church notice boards suggest that Christians are trying actively to discourage others from joining them! The impression is reinforced when there are three huge locked doors to rattle before gaining entry by the smallest which is hidden round the back! Gloves make it hard to turn over the pages of a hymn book but that is sometimes preferable to frost-bite. The lack of decent toilets can embarrass anyone from toddler to visiting preacher! Raising the profile of all-age worship may be helping to speed up some long overdue changes. Many older churches are remodelling their church plant, making better use of space and creating something both attractive and functional: a suitable setting for drama and dance; better lighting and heating and cloakrooms; movable furniture; integrated equipment like overhead projectors and public address sytems; loops for the deaf and disabled access; a refreshments point near the worship area; a corner with toys for children to play quietly; rooms with small tables and chairs. Some churches even stretch to carpet so children can sit or lie on floor: it deadens sound and creates a relaxed atmosphere but can play havoc with the acoustics!

The mere thought of toddlers messing about on the church floor raises an emotive subject. Most of us listen to our gut feelings more than to our heads and everyone has gut feelings about babies! Many are adamant that little children are a noisy distraction, particularly for slightly older children, and should be banished from church until they can understand what is going on. Others argue equally strongly that even the tinies gain spiritually from being with the whole church 'family' and that everyone should bend over backwards to accommodate them. If the presence of both groups is not felt within a congregation then probably one of them has been effectively silenced! Both can become discourteous if they try to impose their views on the other, but learning to listen can be the way to find a useful compromise.

We need to remember that a child's happy noise is part of a congregation's praise to God. However, many parents really cannot worship if they are bothered by a small child and deserve the break of an hour on a Sunday morning. Some defer the decision about creche, happily taking a child into church for months, but suddenly discovering that a quiet baby has turned overnight into an unruly toddler who has never learnt to be left with others. So getting babies used to a creche as young as possible can have enormous advantages. church is an ideal setting for this first stage of separation as parents will always be within easy reach and helpers will be sympathetic. Even children who show distress often settle immediately the parent has left, proving that the parents have the problem, not the child! On the other hand on any one Sunday some children will prefer to stay with parents for all sorts of reasons, and it would be wrong to make such families feel uncomfortable. Hopefully they will be helped to choose the most suitable part of the church; or parents might be encouraged to accompany a child to the appropriate group, particularly during a 'settling in' period.

Wouldn't it be good if every church had a room available where distressed children could be taken, perhaps with sound relayed so that the service can still be heard, or even a video link or soundproof glass? Not all churches will manage this, but it is important to ensure that creche facilities are adequate. There may be local bylaws which require a certain minimum space or adult/child ratio, so this should be researched. A creche is best not located too near the worship area for some parents tend to imagine they hear their own baby crying! On the other hand if it is too far away the helpers might spend all their time walking to and fro trying to contact parents while children are tearful.

Churches who say there is no call for a creche will probably never prove the truth or otherwise of that statement! While it would be foolish to operate an empty creche every week, a shrewd eye needs to be kept on the situation so that something can be arranged the very minute it is needed. churches who have had a vision of more young families being attracted have, in the early days, often run a creche for only one or two clients! Creches, whether staffed by permanent leaders or a rota of parents, are a low-key way for the church to help with parenting and literally a 'Godsend' for the whole congregation!

Hopefully every church has some services at which even the very tiniest are welcome. Our guess is that Jesus would enjoy them wandering round and want them to feel at ease. A child who feels at home in church will in any case be less trouble than one who is on the first visit and cannot help being curious. Adults who value quiet and reverence sometimes fear that toddlers will spoil things, but many children instinctively know when it is right to be silent. When small children are encouraged to come to the front they often behave very well. One church sits its two to four year olds in a group behind the rail which is normally used for the administration of communion in full view of everyone. During open worship they are encouraged to play percussion instruments, but they spontaneously fall silent when the rest of the congregation do so.

All-age all through the week

In Old Testament times it was sometimes hard to distinguish between worship and the tribal 'knees-up'. Our Protestantism can be dry in comparison, obsessed with 'getting it right', strong on piety but short on celebration. Whether directly connected with worship or not, it is impossible to over-emphasise the importance of all-age social events, because faith is nurtured through close human relationships and we only really get close when we 'let our hair down'. As suggested in the previous chapter, social groups are today so polarised that the church may be in a unique position to set an example in bringing the age-groups together.

During the last few decades many congregations have seen the demise of the garden party, the Christmas bazaar, the jumble sale, beetle drives, the Sunday School outing and the pantomime. Sometimes these things have been closed down insensitively, scorned as distractions from the true mission of the church. They did sometimes attain an importance out of all proportion, but they have not always been replaced by events equally successful at drawing people together. Every church needs someone in its leadership team to monitor the overall social planning; to find new and imaginative ways of celebrating the traditional festivals; to capitalise on local and topical events, yet keep such activites in appropriate relationship to the spiritual life of the church.

Events might include days out, treasure hunts, barn dances, barbeques, bonfires, pantomimes, concerts, nearly-new sales, sponsored this and that. Most of these work against stereotyping and provide unique opportunities for adults, particularly the elderly, to meet children; for singles to participate without feeling they should be part of a couple; for the married person with an unsociable partner to have some fun in a safe setting; for neighbours and friends to be brought along for a 'taster' of church life. Teenagers who no longer attend regularly are happy to join in a take-away meal or the parish weekend, still prepared to do an odd job from time to time. church leaders can be recognised as normal human beings and we can all risk being seen without our 'masks'.

Much has been written about the dangers to children in the outside world, but less is said about their need to widen their horizons and experience a world beyond the immediate family. In a church with plenty of interaction between the age-groups, children will have an abundance of teenage and adult role-models and are less likely to be over-protected. Parenting and grandparenting skills will be passed on naturally, something which happens less and less in today's mobile society. Where the 'extended' family lives at the other end of the country, the church often supplies 'substitute' grandparents or nieces and nephews.

Because the 'social' church tends to be an inclusive church it is hard to fix the boundaries between who is 'in' and who is 'out' and this can be a good thing. People can easily stay on the fringe; those with doubts about their faith can make a contribution even when going through a fallow time spiritually. Some whose lifestyles might prevent them from coming to a service because they feel, rightly or wrongly, that they would be put under moral scrutiny can also find themselves at ease in these situations – the unmarried couple with their children, the divorced man or woman, the blended family, the homosexual couple. It allows a church to say, 'God is at work in your lives and we want you to meet Jesus', instead of the message which is so often communicated, 'You must change to our standards before you are allowed in'.

Of course we will be wary of turning the church into a club. Also some people do not want the church as the hub of their social life and we must not make them feel excluded because they only come to Sunday services. But any group, including the nuclear family, is healthier when it does a whole range of activities together. We all need to belong to something larger than family yet small enough for us to grow in the security of close relationships.

3
FROM THEORY TO PRACTICE

Something marvellous happened in a south London church one Sunday not so long ago. The speaker was making her way through her prepared all-age talk about forgiveness. It was a good, short, unspectacular talk, but it was quite clear that, four minutes in, she had completely lost the attention of the congregation. This was because a toddler had made his way to the front of the room and, oblivious to the fact that every eye was on him, was pulling the cloth that covered the table on which bread and wine were waiting for later use. Not even an expert preacher can compete with the shared mounting expectation of a catastrophe! Seeing what was happening out of the corner of her eye, the speaker moved slowly and reassuringly toward the child, not pausing for a moment in what she said. She swept him up in her arms and continued her talk with the boy perched on one hip. Astonished by the attention, the toddler gazed up at her and began to listen intently to every word she said – so the speaker brought the talk to a close by addressing what she had to say about the richness of God's love and mercy to him quietly and personally. By this stage the rest of the congregation were paying rapt attention to everything that was going on, and were straining their ears in earnest silence so as not to miss a word that was said. No planned activity in the church that year was as moving or reassuring as that spontaneous visual aid of God's loving and personal rescue. It was the very best of all-age worship . . . and it will never happen again!

Structured and unstructured worship

Readers of this book will fall into two categories, or possibly three. There will be those whose favoured form of service follows the same pattern week-in, week-out, usually making use of a prepared order and prayers, some of which are written out to be spoken corporately (structured, or 'liturgical' worship). Others will prefer a service in which little has been planned (except perhaps the sermon, a Bible reading or anything else that is a special feature of that particular service) and God is invited to lead the congregation to contribute and participate in any way which pleases him (unstructured, or 'Spirit-led' worship). The possible third category consists of those who prefer not to have a written order for their service, but who have found a particular pattern of activity so helpful over the years that they have developed an unstated structure which they might even deny having! All-age worship is well suited to all of these patterns, but. . . .

For churches which have a well-established ministry among adults there is an obstacle to overcome when trying to develop all-age work. It is this! All-age worship is not adult worship at which children happen to be present. Neither is it children's worship at which adults are observers. It is something different. At its best it has features which can only take place when children and adults are in the same room at the same time.

It is unhelpful to think about all-age worship by starting with a successful adult form of service, be it structured or unstructured, and working out how children can be squeezed into that format; along that path sit children who have brought comics to read quietly while activities take place which they do not recognise as being meant for them. And equally there is little to be gained by squeezing adults into the kind of programme which is loved by children's groups; many adults don't even try to sit along that path, they walk away unsatisfied.

The sad truth is that an exciting adult service is as likely to produce bored children as a dull adult service! Bringing in a drum kit does not make an adult service suitable for all ages. Adding a children's talk does not make an adult service suitable for all ages. Worship that meets the desire of many generations to bring their own needs and the needs of the world before God begins when leaders ask themselves: How can we make best use of the special dynamic created by putting adults and children next to each other, while staying faithful to the tradition to which we belong?

For those with a structured service, the first step almost invariably involves loosening some of the structures. For example, a prayer which is long and has many clauses is a huge obstacle for children to climb over: even if every individual word is comprehensible to children who can read, the cumulative impact of a long prayer is so unlike anything else in childhood experience that they assume it is not meant for them. There should be other opportunities in church life for adults alone to use these prayers which are so precious to their spirituality, but when children are present there are different ways to pray in which the whole congregation can approach God as one.

Equally, those with an unstructured service may need to introduce some structure by asking the Spirit to lead their thinking and their organisation during the week before as well as during the service. For example, if a decision is made to use some of the more creative approaches to thanksgiving (so helpful to those whose mastery of words is still developing), a basic amount of preparation needs to happen in advance since someone needs to bring pencils and paper!

Patterns of leadership

Much of the tone of an all-age service is set by the way its leader addresses a congregation. A leader whose greeting indicates to every generation present that they are welcome gains the confidence of children and adults alike from the very start and signals the fact that their needs are going to be met in a relevant way. However, those who talk to adults in a mercilessly mature tone and vocabulary over the heads of children (sometimes literally) send out a signal that it is time for that section of the congregation to switch off their attention. The tone that encourages an intergenerational group to worship is the tone of a family meal table at its best – warm, considerate, serious sometimes and light at others, but never telling children to shut up and eat because the grown ups are talking! Just as children come to realise that they are going to have to stop playing football while they eat, they will also come to realise that an all-age service is never going to be a free-for-all runaround (although hopefully there will be other opportunities in the church's life for this kind of activity). But if what they see and hear is constantly engaging for them, the disapproving glare from an interrupted worshipper should be a rarity!

The atmosphere in the minutes before a service begins can greatly help both children and adults to prepare for worship. Silence is very threatening, but music (perhaps a group singing less familiar songs that the congregation will later join in) can help move people gently from the chattery pleasure of greeting friends to an expectation of meeting God. Calm is desirable (rather than a last-minute adjustment of furniture or microphones), and all kinds of visual interest help to focus attention. They can allow parents the opportunity to point out colours, light, symbols, candles, flowers, banners and so on to their children. And in that spirit, the congregation is ready to start worship at the same time that the leader is!

The choice of who leads all-age worship is in itself a statement about its recognised value. It is sometimes the case that the person who usually leads adult worship is not particularly gifted at working in a multi-generation context, and leaders who are both humble and visionary enough to recognise this in themselves rightly choose to delegate leadership of all or parts of services such as these to others who have appropriate talents. However, it is most important that this is not seen to confer second-best status on intergenerational work. The church's overall leaders need to show that they own all-age worship as a mainstream part of church activity. The position they stand in and the way they participate indicates this more clearly than a hundred verbal assurances of its value. So, for example, if a song which has actions has been chosen, the leader should either introduce and 'conduct' it himself, or should take part fully under someone else's leadership as a sign that this is the expected level of participation of everyone present, both young and old.

One candidate for the worst expression of children's worth came in a church in Scotland (but it could have been anywhere). After leading twenty minutes of activity with children and adults together (which, to be fair, was not in any sense boring), the minister announced, 'Right, we'll let the children go now'. They filed out in sombre silence. When they had gone the man brushed his hands together like a cook dusting the last, nasty bits of dough off his hands after mixing pastry and said, 'Good, now let's get on with it!' Perhaps the adults wished they had left with the children! Or perhaps he was merely verbalising what others before and since have silently thought.

If the preparation of all-age worship is in the hands of one man or woman, it allows a consistent style to develop, which is helpful for those in the congregation whose major problem with enjoying it is its unpredictability. It also allows for a controlled and specific delegation of responsibility, with particular people and groups being given a chance to exercise and develop the gifts that God has given them. The disadvantage of having a single leader is that it can become an onerous task unless he or she has access to imaginative resources and a steady flow of stimuli. Some churches involve a group of people in the planning of this kind of worship, and often leaders of children's groups are part of this – sometimes even older children themselves. The advantage of bringing many minds together is obvious, but it does involve extremely time-consuming meetings, especially if there is some element of all-age worship every week. It can also lead to a hotch-potch service in which everyone's idea is thrown into the casserole without much thought given to the overall flavour or blend. And if there is an attempt to short cut the time involved by delegating planning to a different group each time, it is very hard to maintain any consistency either in content or in quality.

One solution is to establish a loose order of events which is standardised over a long period, ensuring that within it there is ample space to invite the participation of many different people or groups. This minimises logistic difficulty but maximises potential for creative involvement. In that spirit, there are three patterns of service offered in the resource section of this book, two for structured services and one for an unstructured one.

Style

Long experience has led to four rules of thumb for the style of successful all-age worship. They do not encompass everything that could be said, but they have proved memorable and valuable to many people:

1. **It is simple.** This is not the same as saying that it is trivial. The truths deep at the heart of the Christian faith *are* simple.

It is not only important for children to discover them for the first time, it is sometimes good for adults to peel away the complications that accumulate as we think deeply about what we believe and rediscover the directness of God's dealings with his people. And of course, for both adults and children arriving in a church for the first time with the barest grasp of religious understanding, simplicity is essential.

Rejoicing that God loves us is a simple activity. Saying sorry for wrong thoughts, words and actions is a simple activity. Praying for people who are sick to be made well is a simple activity. And so is hearing the timeless story of what Jesus did. There is more to be investigated about grace, about sin, about healing, and about Christology – but on other occasions. When adults and children are together simple truths can come shining through the mists like a beacon.

2. **It is not childish**. In particular, it is not embarrassing for adults. This is the corollary of the first rule of thumb. The object of putting adults, teenagers and children together is categorically not that adults should pretend to be kiddies – even those adults who enjoy 'making fools of themselves'. We go to public worship ready to meet God as we are, not wearing a mask. We go as sinful people ready to be forgiven, we go as humble people ready to thank and praise, and we go as expectant people ready to learn. If we are encouraged to go and disguise ourselves as children we are off the hook, and we will not be able to meet with God in the way he desires. This means that everything that is offered to the congregation for their participation must be presented in such a way that no one feels belittled by it.

This by no means rules out movement during songs – but it does mean that the congregation should be invited to join in as a way of offering their whole body in praise, rather than required to do so as a way of partying in God's presence. It means that when pencils and paper are given out at the beginning of a time of prayer, drawing is encouraged as an option for those who find it easier than writing, not insisted on as a jolly way of having fun with God. Teenagers in particular need to find in all-age worship the freedom to be themselves, not the pressure to be adult beyond their years nor the embarrassment of being identified as children.

3. **It is visual where possible**. In this generation, members of

churches need visual stimuli not because they are children, but because they are human!

Ours is not the first generation for which this is true. In past centuries church leaders had to respond to the problem that many members of their congregations were illiterate. So they taught by filling their walls with murals and their windows with stained glass. The problem for this generation is not so much illiteracy (although with 12% of adults having little or no reading it is quite wrong to say this lightly), it is the increasingly limited concentration span caused and fed off by television-watching. Not only teaching but also our prayers and our praise can be enhanced, as later chapters of this book suggest, by meeting this 'picture generation' with the culture to which it is accustomed. It is our privilege to be able to respond not only with stained glass, but also with the overhead projector, with puppets, with visual aids, with drama, with video, with banners, with drawings and symbols, with flowers, with. . . .

4. **It is interactive where possible**. By this two things are meant. First there is interaction between the leader of the service and the congregation. Prayers in which the congregation respond to the leader, sometimes with a repeated line of praise, thanksgiving or request, are tremendously helpful for children. They allow them to participate even if they cannot fully understand the intricacies of the prayer or are unable to read. They also create a rhythm, which heightens the impact of a prayer among the congregation (not, of course, to God), and encourage simplicity. And those qualities are not only important for children, they are valuable to adults. Many such prayers appear in the resource section of this book. In all-age teaching, too, the value of interaction is great. Informal comments and questions which invite a reply increase attention and raise the expectation that what is said will be relevant.

Second there is interaction among the congregation itself. It has become commonplace to hear people say that adults learn as much from children as children learn from adults. However, simply to put different generations in the same room does not guarantee that such learning will take place. It is only when congregations are offered activities which cross the generations that it can be achieved. There is a huge potential for learning hidden within the words, 'Turn to the people you are sitting next to, adults and children together, and talk about. . .'. This may take some getting used to for congregations who are new to it – what usually happens is that children leap to it enthusiastically, but adults find themselves taken by surprise that their opinions are being sought. It is vital to offer an opt-out, ('If you prefer to think about it quietly by yourself, that is fine'), to explain the instructions carefully, ('Swivel on your seats or pews so that you can talk comfortably to the two or three people next to you'), and to make sure that no one is unintentionally excluded, ('If you are with friends or family, look round to see whether anyone would like to join your conversation'). This cannot work if the congregation is always asked to sit in age-segregated groups, for example with the children's groups sitting in a different area of the church from the adults, but it can be pointed out that there is much to be gained from sharing in this way, ('If you are fortunate enough to have children in your cluster make sure you listen to what they say, and, boys and girls, if you are lucky enough to have grown ups next to you be sure to ask them what they think').

The kinds of question that help people learn in these settings are open-ended ones – those which ask for an opinion or give a chance to share experience, ('Tell the others in your group about a time when you prayed for something and God answered' or, 'What could each of you do this week to show that what God has taught you today will make a difference to your lives?') On one occasion in an inner London church, the preacher stopped what he had to say about the challenge of being a Christian and asked the congregation to cluster and talk about what they find difficult about trying to follow Jesus. In one group a fourteen-year-old girl described what it was like to be the only Christian she knew of in a vast, tough school. An eighty-year-old lady sat opposite with her eyes wide open and commented, 'I had no idea that schools were like that these days; I admire you so much for living as a Christian in those circumstances.' She then went on to talk about her experience of being a Christian during the War, and it was the turn of the girl to sit spellbound as she was led into a world she might never otherwise have encountered. This pricelessly valuable learning could never have taken place if the preacher had gone on speaking for his allotted time, no matter how fine his oratory. It was genuinely intergenerational learning. Something like it could happen in any church in the country – next Sunday!

Content

In some respects, the content of all-age worship is dictated by the tradition to which a church belongs. Structured services still largely reflect the intentions of the Protestant reformers that the order should be: awareness of God's presence, confession, praise, Bible reading, statement of belief, intercessory prayer, teaching (the order being slightly different at a communion service). This has a pleasing theological logic to it, and there is much to be said for following that pattern, even if each element is expressed in an entirely new way. It brings with it some problems, though. If the practice of a church is to have children and adults together for the first part of a service before separating for peer group teaching, at what point do the children leave?

It is good for children to see the whole range of expression to God that makes up the worship of the church. When all generations are together for a whole service, children need to glimpse everything into which they are growing – including prayer, teaching, baptism and communion. When children are present only for part of the service, it is helpful to work out how they can experience all these things over the course of time. Perhaps appropriately simple songs of praise can be sung before they leave, followed by more complex songs when only adults are left to appreciate them fully. Many churches like to offer a short talk or learning activity for both children and adults when they are together, before having a more developed sermon for adults while children are elsewhere for teaching at their own level. This works exceptionally well in the visionary churches which have brought their adult and children's programmes in line thematically, since it can introduce the subject that all will be following in their own way in different rooms.

In churches where adults and children begin apart, but join together towards the end of a service, there is a great opportunity to respond to what has been learnt (again, particularly if everyone has been following the same theme) in thanksgiving, praise or even confession, perhaps culminating in the communion which unites a church. At this time, children could show to the adult congregation the models they have made, the drama they have prepared or the new songs they have learnt – all presented as their contribution to the shared worship of those present. Someone could also explain to the children what the grown ups have been learning about so as to give them a sense of the adult life of the church in which we long that they will one day participate.

When a service consists of many elements in this way, it is important that one person has overall control of where the service is heading in order to allow it to flow. Some problems can be anticipated and avoided in advance. For example, although many churches find a quiz to be a popular element of all-age worship (it is, after all, involving and can be used to reinforce past teaching), it is virtually impossible to place it in a service without a wrench of mood. To move from a reflective song of submission to a competitive frolic of questions and answers helps no-one. Likewise, to follow the thundering excitement of the quiz by saying, 'And now let us pray', is usually unsatisfactory. A service needs to build towards a certain point, and then to relax from it. The climax need not be the teaching – it could be a prayerful response to the teaching, or the communion, or the commissioning of someone for a new task in God's service. However, the order of what happens must rise and fall in a suitable way – not tumble together like a series of happenings in no particular order. Children are no better at swinging their moods instantly than adults – both need to be helped into God's immediate presence, to be aware of what is going on between him and them, and then to have their attention directed outward to the world into which they are going to walk with him.

Much of this applies to unstructured services also. Many people testify to the blessing they receive through hearing children praise God simply and directly, and the healing and reassurance that has come through the prayers of children. However, in order to release this, most children need to have confidence that what they offer is both acceptable and valued. There are several things which hinder children from opening themselves to God when adults are present. One is not realising what is going on – so leaders of all-age worship in this context need to spell out very clearly what their expectations are at each point in the service in a very straightforward way and in more detail than they would if only adults were present. For example, knowing that children find it relatively easy to thank God for things that are important to them, it may be good to open one part of the service strictly to thanksgiving alone – this is not stifling the leading of the Holy Spirit, but widening the range of people through whom the Spirit can work.

Another difficulty for children is seeing and hearing role-models whom they cannot emulate. If they hear adults offering long, complex prayers to God, whether it is in tongues or in a language they can understand, children will assume that only length and complexity are acceptable. Many churches, have found that even if it is stated clearly that simple prayers are welcome from children, they feel unable to take part because what they observe speaks more powerfully than what they are told. It is quite possible that in another setting where only children are present they will say the prayer that God had been prompting in them – too late for adults to share in the blessing that came from it.

There are several ways of approaching this when it happens. The first is direct teaching to adults about why children are present and what the whole congregation must do to make worship accessible to them – the limitations they must put on themselves about the music they choose, the length and style of the prayers they say, and the appropriateness of the sharing that takes place (for some adults, this may require a personal word-in-the-ear). More detailed advice is given in chapter 7. This kind of approach takes several weeks to get used to, but is worth striving for. It means that in one North England church, after half-an-hour of bored inattention to theologically complex songs and prayers and the gynaecological details of someone's pregnancy, a twelve-year-old will never again have to leave for his children's group whispering to a complete stranger, 'Bet you wish you could escape too!'

In both structured and unstructured services, the leader needs to be aware of and sensitive to time. It is not only difficult for children when a service stretches beyond their natural span of comfort, it is also hard for the adults who have brought them. If all generations are together for the whole service, it is difficult to see any justification for it going on for more than an hour – and unless there is a good deal of involving activity, it may be that fifty to fifty-five minutes is a more appropriate length. This should not be a problem in unstructured services, for the Holy Spirit is perfectly capable of leading us graciously in a quite concise way – unless we are deaf to him and assume that only length counts to our timeless God. However, churches which have a structure that consistently pushes the length over an hour need to look carefully at whether everything in their structure is so important that it must take place every time – unless contented toddlers and senior citizens alike are so engaged that they ask for more!

When the service falls into two parts – one with adults and children together and one with them apart – the break between the sections allows a little more leeway in timing. Perhaps seventy minutes is acceptable (twenty-five minutes together, a five-minute break, forty minutes separately), depending on whether the programme on offer to the different groups fills that time with appropriate activity that absorbs the attention of those involved. It is, however, important to remember that among those in the congregation will be very young children, and it is damaging to separate them from their parents for too long – how devastating it is for a pre-school child to learn that church is the place where week-by-week she goes in order to cry because her father or mother is kept from her. Or for a baby to learn that church is the only place where he isn't fed when he is hungry and must wait in discomfort when he is wet. When judging an appropriate time-scale, don't forget that an all-age church is an *all*-age church!

Evaluation

The wisdom of evaluating church activity is not restricted only to all-age worship, but perhaps it is particularly important since it is attempting to cater for so many different needs. It is important to ask for the help of a cross-section of people involved both as leaders and participants, since unsolicited comments only usually come from those with particularly strong opinions, often negative ones. This checklist might help as a starting point for reviewing a particular service, which could lead to wider reflection on the whole range of provision for intergenerational activity. Everyone who fills in the questionnaire should give a mark from nought to five for each category:

Did the service as a whole . . .

1 Express a biblical truth?

2 Encourage people to listen to and learn from God?

3 Encourage people to approach God in praise, intercession, repentance, and so on?

4 Flow from one item to the next?

5 Allow for different levels of understanding?

6 Allow for different spans of concentration?

7 Involve the participation of people of all ages?

8 Allow movement?

9 Enable people to learn and worship by looking as well as hearing?

10 Enable people to learn and worship by doing as well as hearing?

11 Contain something appropriate for every age?

12 Help everyone to feel welcome, at ease and accepted regardless of their age, marital status, familiarity with church life, and so on?

Which numbers were given four or five points by the majority of people? We need to build on these strengths. How?

Which numbers were given two or three points? Could we improve on what is proving generally acceptable? How?

Which numbers scored nought or one? We need to act quickly. How?

4
WORSHIP IS NOT A SPECTATOR SPORT!

Worship is not just entertainment. In the early days of 'family services' parents were present almost as 'guests' and much of the participation was of the 'performance' variety. Sometimes today all-age worship is criticised for being 'a show' with the leader simply a 'compere' figure. Of course it is all right to enjoy ourselves in church and to experiment with new things in worship. Games and prizes, balloons and party-poppers all have their place, so long as they are kept in it! Unusual ideas are useful if they catch the imagination and draw people into what is going on; but they are a hindrance if they distract and trivialise, and give confusing or even incorrect messages about God.

Those of us with good experiences of children's worship are probably convinced that participation is desirable, even essential. However, this chapter is certainly not about people doing embarrassing things for the sake of the children. Rather it is about using our imagination to recognise the whole range of new and old ways that worshippers can take part. Indeed, participation is implicit in all good worship.

Worship is work

'Liturgy' means 'the work of the people'. All worship requires everyone to make some effort. A useful analogy is cooking alongside children. For some adults such 'work' is an enormously exciting and stimulating experience; for others it feels like toil and is desperately untidy and frustrating. People who always need a 'right' way of doing things may concentrate on teaching the 'rules', perhaps feeling deep down that children cannot really join in until they have grasped them. There is some truth in that, but in both activities we would do well to remember that there is no one correct way; just a few tried and tested tips to keep in mind as we get on and do the work for ourselves.

So we do not learn to cook or to worship by watching. We have all experienced worship where the congregation are spectators for everything except the hymns; and this can happen in informal preaching services and very slick all-age events as well as in choral evensong! Of course quite often, though we show few outward signs of participation, our minds are working overtime. We may be processing the erudite information from someone else's talk or silently agreeing with the content of their prayers. Participation is not confined to what goes on in our heads, however, and accepting children at their own faith level will mean adapting our cerebral ways of 'working'.

Neither is participation confined to what happens between 10 and 11am, or whatever is the service time! One concept implicit in the idea of 'children's church' was that of children taking the roles of church 'officers'. This was good but, of course, restricted to their own events and limited in its effect. Nowadays children can take their place alongside adults in serving the congregation: setting out the chairs, greeting people at the door, handing out books, taking the collection, making the bread and wine ready for use, setting out and serving refreshments. Some churches officially 'elect' whole families as sidespeople or stewards during an annual meeting; others use children on their own for special services.

Worship is staying in my seat!

Tried and tested ways of participation include hymns and songs; psalms, prayers, chants and readings with simple responses. Thought needs to be given as to the best way of presenting any words we want the congregation to read out. Obviously they may be in a book, printed out specially or displayed clearly at the front; but in addition it is sometimes possible to teach them orally, particularly if they are quite brief. It is important for children to learn to use the written word in worship, but best not to include too many activities from which non-readers will feel excluded. Those who lead informal worship need to remember that children usually need very obvious cues for speaking out loud, as do many adults!

It does not spoil the fun of cooking if only adults are allowed to use the sharpest knife or put the cake in the oven. It is inevitable that some things in church are only suitable for older children and adults, particularly if the main worship event every week is all-age. There is no reason why little children cannot occasionally be given something else to do, such as drawing a picture or doing a simple puzzle on the notice sheet during long items. However, if this were to happen every week, it would defeat the object of all-age worship and give children the strong message that it is acceptable not to concentrate in church.

Many churches invite anyone from the congregation to join in quite long periods of open worship, including the use of spiritual gifts. The blessing of seeing children participate at this time is great because of its directness and spontaneity. Their simple approach may occasionally allow God to lead a congregation in a way that adult complexity would overlook. However, sometimes children are able to worship freely in their own groups but the presence of the whole church is just too much! Where the atmosphere of the church is genuinely and consistently conducive to all-age participation, these problems may soon disappear and children will join in quite naturally. On the other hand it is important to remember that children can be extremely embarrassed at things their parents do, and the refusal to conform is often a simple sign of growing up, not a rejection of what is actually happening. It is also worth asking a group of children what they perceive to be happening and what would help them to join in more – the answers might be very illuminating!

Worship is getting up out of my seat!

During the last two or three decades many more people have been encouraged to read the Bible aloud or lead prepared prayers. In most churches, on the average Sunday, several men and women will share the task of leading parts of the worship with the minister. This is a good development because children now see it as a natural thing to do and any contribution they make is less conspicuous than in the past. When selecting children to take part like this we must resist the temptation to single out the 'stars'. The extrovert will always volunteer but the introvert may do an equally good job, given sufficient encouragement.

All-age worship provides 'one-off' opportunities for individuals and groups who would not normally take a lead. In some churches it is quite usual to see children's groups leading prayers or songs, or doing a reading or short play, but other organised groups, such as a parent-and-toddler club, a Mothers' Union, house group, or even a badminton or football club, can do the same. Particularly effective is a contribution from a group of teenagers. Many simple things do not need rehearsing, such as holding up pictures, reading a very simple script, or representing the characters in a story by wearing simple 'costumes' such as labels or appropriate hats.

Though we want to do our best for God, what happens in church does not need to be perfect. Children who are seen to be involved in leading worship are the same as inexperienced adults. They need guidance and practice, but it might be counter-productive to demand a polished performance. The greatest problem with inexperienced people is making sure they can be heard! Ideally, large buildings will have a public address system, though some instruction is necessary for people to feel comfortable using it. Almost all children speak more quickly 'on the day' than when practising, but rather than over-rehearse, think carefully about where they stand, whether the material is really appropriate, and how it could be reinforced either visually or by being repeated in another form.

Children certainly do not need to be applauded. Occasionally this will happen spontaneously and clapping is in many places a frequent ingredient in worship. But try to find ways which affirm, yet avoid the suggestion of competition or performance. Best of all involve children and adults together, for example a family could be invited to lead a time of prayer, each contributing a prayer in language which comes naturally to them. Better still – a group that mixes a family with single people! Within reasonable limits we can risk involving children in things they cannot understand; indeed in worship most of us use concepts which we are only just beginning to grasp!

Leading music is an ideal situation for the generations to work together as a team. It may be impracticable for children to take a full part in the church's music, but they could join in the leadership of one song or group of songs per week, just participate occasionally, or be invited to play percussion instruments without rehearsal. Similarly they can be involved with drama, mime or dance groups. A certain flexibility in the membership of such groups can be a healthy thing for it guards against them becoming too autonomous and too 'professional'.

Worship is belonging to a tradition

A family were sight-seeing several years ago in a large cathedral. It was a cold and windy day and eight-year-old Simon was zipped into a warm anorak. As they passed the verger he rudely pulled down Simon's hood and angrily muttered something about respect for God. The family, not sure how to react, walked on in embarrassment. The parents' anger began to rise as they felt the insult on Simon's behalf. Here was a regular church-goer, a young Christian who knew God in his own way, who behaved with due reverence in their church building at home. Not even possessing a real hat, he could not have known not to wear it in church! Of course mum and dad probably had their own agenda; a sense of guilt at not doing one's duty as a good Christian parent; an urge to be defiant in the face of the stuffiest extreme of the church of England!

Years later the incident is just a tiny painful memory, but it has something to teach us about tradition. God may not sit in heaven checking out what little boys wear, but he has given human beings the ability to invent all kinds of symbols to help them approach him with reverence. We have no right to scorn things which are important to others and, though we need not conform ourselves, by doing so we might get new insights about God. Most children are raised in the preferred tradition of their parents, but we must consider what 'message' our congregation gives about other parts of the church. When teenagers and young adults get to the stage of struggling to express the faith in their own way, it is helpful for them to have access to other resources.

This is equally true for many adults in mid-life, who have known only one style of church. It is no good saying that what really matters is knowing God personally, for in practice none of us separates personal faith from church 'culture'. No matter what tradition we are raised in, it takes an act of will to shake off the message we can implicitly absorb – that God really does prefer to work through *our* sort of church. Living at a time when there is much cross-fertilisation of ideas between Christians of different denominations and churchmanship, we are in a better position to avoid passing on our prejudices to our children. Simon's parents had no strong opinions about hats being worn in church, but thank goodness they did not over-react to the verger's words, for his reaction may have signified something very important for him.

From that same cathedral visit came another lesson. A workman doing repairs gave Simon a lump of ancient stone to take home and keep. The family do not collect religious artifacts and it probably got thrown out long ago, but at the time it had meaning, reminding them that Christian worship had gone on in that place for many centuries, and linking the worship of the past with that of the present. So another thing we can say about participation in worship is that it is not just something that happens at weekly gatherings in our own location. It means belonging to the whole church, the 'catholic' or universal church. It is as if we are playing in just one scene of a huge drama that goes on for all time. We know few details of the other scenes which continually play all round the world, but now and again it is good to remind each other that there is a common theme to them all.

Worship is using all our senses

For those of us whose Christianity is mostly in our heads, 'concrete' expressions of worship can be immensely helpful in opening up new ways to God. We can consciously enjoy touching not only bits of the building, but another person's hand, a palm cross, or something from creation such as a stone or a leaf. We can use our other senses, too. Looking at banners, pictures, stained-glass windows, flower arrangements, a burning candle, the colours of vestments, hands lifted high in praise, the shading of old stone walls: listening to new sounds, instruments, songs, the noises outside, even the silence: smelling a flower or a leaf, the musty hymn book or our neighbour or even incense! Tasting usually comes with holy communion or afterwards with the refreshments, but the imaginative can find ways of integrating even this! In all these ways the whole congregation participates without words and without rehearsal.

We can also encourage people to use their bodies in movement: not only action choruses but simple dance, hand movements both led and impromptu, kneeling, bowing, the sign of the cross. Processions can involve presenting harvest gifts or collecting a lighted candle or moving round to pray in different parts of the building such as around a notice board which displays information about overseas links. Used as a 'one-off', any of these things can enrich worship and need not be adopted every week. Many of these ideas, and those in the creative worship section at the end of this book, will help people get in touch with their feelings, and this needs to be acknowledged verbally. Leaders need to choose words which reassure people that it is not unusual to cry or laugh, yet do not draw undue attention to individuals.

Worship is about my sort of church

People's willingness to participate will vary from congregation to congregation. Some say they come to church to be on their own with God. Some seem compelled to criticise when any new idea is introduced. Sometimes plans which are agreed never seem to take off. All-age enthusiasts who become frustrated with those who resist change must try to understand why this is so.

Churches fall into two broad types; those where most of the members live in the immediate vicinity, (sometimes called 'community' churches), and those which attract men and women from a wide area who want to be with like-minded people (sometimes called 'gathered' churches). Examples of both are found throughout the denominations, though the latter is more common in the evangelical and charismatic churches. Because of its responsibility for a parish, an Anglican church might represent the 'community' model; an independent evangelical church, being fairly autonomous, the 'gathered' type. There are of course many exceptions and often the two are combined in one congregation. Because it is hard to define the boundaries of the first, it is sometimes criticised for preaching a 'social Gospel'. The weakness of the second is that it can attract people so unanimous in belief and preferred worship style that different opinions may go unheard. The 'community' church is often better at 'taking the rough with the smooth', the 'gathered' church more likely to deal with conflict by splitting.

Deciding which 'label' fits our own church can help us understand people's attitudes and decide how to encourage more participation. If the leadership of a 'gathered' church is committed to all-age worship it will probably succeed; if not it may never even get discussed. Once participation of any sort is seen as permissible, folk will conform or opt out totally. For instance, in this sort of church every person might seem to enjoy putting their hands in the air! The danger is that enthusiastic leaders may lose the restraining voices that maintain a sense of proportion in decision-making. The 'community' model with its wider mix of people can give more opportunities for gentle experimentation. For instance, the 'parade' services in Anglican and Methodist churches have for years provided acceptable outlets for all-age ideas. At the same time, and working against change, the traditions of these denominations may prevent such ideas being used more widely.

Worship is about using symbols

We cannot avoid symbols because we are using them whether we realise it or not. They are a kind of shorthand, eloquent when words might be difficult or slow or insensitive. Even those who think they have stripped their Christianity bare by avoiding the rituals of the past, like the iconoclastic Puritans of the fifteenth century, quickly re-invent symbols such as the 'right' hymns, or mannerisms, or religious jargon. A current example is the popularity of the fish sign. In evangelical circles the Bible itself is a powerful symbol which sometimes acquires a life of its own.

Throughout history God has chosen to communicate in symbols and the Bible is rich in powerful images such as light, fire, water and oil. Nowadays, to prevent these becoming too messy, they may be transformed into something tidy and ecclesiastical; clean-burning candles, pre-heated baptismal pools, and oil in a nice little cosmetic jar! Hopefully we will enjoy using symbols whilst always being on our guard lest they become more important than what they symbolise. They help engage all the senses and also the emotions; they communicate truth and encourage faith on the intuitive level. They help worship to address the whole person, all people and at all times. The 'cerebral' Christian can find symbols threatening because they can't be controlled like words. They are certainly risky, for each person will interpret them slightly differently, sometimes in what we think is the 'wrong way'!

In all-age worship symbols are tremendously useful and slightly dangerous. Useful because involving the whole person is particularly desirable when the intellectual ability of some of the participants is limited; dangerous because, if children are not taught what a symbol means, in adult life it will become either a breeding ground for superstition or something trivial to be rejected. All-age worship can be an ideal place to explain symbols, because the need for simple but explicit language challenges the leader to think out exactly what their purpose is. One church used an Advent wreath for the first time, each week progressively lighting the five candles and hearing an explanation about the build-up to Christmas and the symbolism of Christ as the 'light of the world'. The fact that a lively toddler blew the candles out on one occasion accidently reminded everyone that they were just candles! For this congregation it may not be appropriate to repeat the idea every year, yet symbolism has been used very effectively. A less traditional way to handle a classic idea is to hand over to God our pain or confusion, quite literally by writing or drawing on small pieces of paper and placing them in a symbolic setting such as at the foot of a cross.

Worship is about becoming dependent

Adults need to get in touch with the 'child' inside them, to step out of their role as people who are coping well with life and slip for a while into dependence. It is natural and healthy for us to alternate frequently between being self-reliant and reliant on something or someone else. The framework of worship allows us to do this together for it can provide ways of handling our anxiety and help us replenish our resources. This is why it is important that we start to rely on symbols, for thinking then becomes less important and imagination and feelings come into their own. This happens in all churches, not just those which talk about symbolism. We must give some thought as to what are the powerful, but perhaps unacknowledged, symbols for our congregation and whether they are doing their job.

If we are not given the opportunity to manage the pain and confusion we carry in varying degrees by means of symbols, we may fail to 'engage' in worship at all. We recognise this in people who often remain on the outside of worship, perhaps feeling very negative about the church's style. Rather than expecting ourselves to cut off from the outside world the minute we enter church, the early part of a service needs to include some acknowledgement of all the 'agendas' being carried. One obvious way of doing this is a prayer of confession, but it can be achieved with music, an informal word, a symbolic action, or a psalm which expresses people's moods. Toward the end of worship the opposite must happen, for we need to be moved away from the symbols we are relying on and into the 'real world' again. The Anglican communion service achieves this with the words, 'Go in peace to love and serve the Lord. In the name of Christ, Amen.' The same sentiments can be expressed in many other ways.

Normally we do not lose our sense of reality throughout this process. We can always distinguish between objects and what they symbolise, such as the bread and wine and the idea of receiving Christ in communion. However, it is possible to be so 'sucked into' worship that fantasy and reality are confused, and it is hard to emerge. If we get 'hooked' on symbols rather than on what is being symbolised, our thinking becomes distorted. For instance we might adopt an almost 'superstitious' attitude to the sacraments, the supernatural, tiny details of worship, or the taintedness of the world outside. We might rely too much on the leader, or the building, or what the church's founder said, or our favourite doctrine, rather than taking on as part of ourselves the values they represent and integrating them into our everyday life.

So it is normal to become childlike in worship, but it is also normal to emerge as adult Christians once again. Many people, who seem very competent in everyday life, enjoy the dependency of worship so much that they are reluctant to risk any change. At the same time, others will be feeling as if they are always poised on the edge of worship, never getting anything from it. Neither group should surprise us. As worship leaders we need to think carefully about what we hope will happen for people at each stage of a service, and find acceptable ways of enabling this to take place.

Worship is joining in

So all-age worship is not a spectator sport. Joining in can be both hard work and great fun. It may mean change for people set in their ways, a new respect for tradition for those who see themselves as modern, a letting-go into dependency for the self-sufficient. Worship is about using our senses, using symbols, using our whole selves to engage with God.

But churches are different and participation can mean different things. What works in one church cannot be forced on another. Individuals vary, too. They come to church for all kinds of reasons, and at any one time many different things may be going on in people's lives of which we are totally unaware. There will always be some who are in too fragile a state to be challenged, and for them participation may be very threatening. We must learn tact as we invite people to do things, not demand their participation. A non-participatory alternative such as 'just sit still and pray silently about it', can be offered as equally valid. Certainly the situation should never arise where anyone is forced to join in or be made to feel they are the odd one out.

Participation in worship requires a lot of sensitivity and a lot of risk. The balance between what we do and what God does is never easy to find, and ultimately, whether worship works depends on the free gift of God's grace. But he will honour our willingness to throw our whole selves into worship, to stretch our meagre resources in finding new ways to give him worth.

5
GIVING AN
ALL-AGE TALK

Many eloquent preachers are terrified at the thought of giving an all-age talk. Those for whom expository preaching has always been the high spot of the service can find it hard to adjust to a 'mixed' audience. Some say it is impossible to address different generations simultaneously; that all-age sermons are really directed at those aged 'about seven'. Other speakers are more positive, glad of the excuse to spell out basic truths to adults. In the past, some denominations supplemented the 'real' sermon with a 'children's address' after which children left or settled down to inevitable boredom. Though this pattern has been criticised, it is now seriously suggested that adults gained a lot from it. It certainly helped introduce new ideas into church and encouraged the element of teaching within preaching. It seems that our attention span is getting less and less, and that television is training both children and adults to expect a change every two-and-a-half minutes! Perhaps we can risk letting things run on a little longer than that, but it does seem that the ability to listen to long traditional sermons can no longer be seen as a prerequisite for Christian maturity. Perhaps the creative all-age approach is just what is needed in the ailing church today.

How people learn

The last fifty years have seen huge changes in our understanding about the way both children and adults learn. Different people learn in different ways, an obvious truth that has not been grasped by many who teach in church! At an all-age service we might be addressing young children who experience the world through their senses; older children who can retain facts but have not reached the stage of abstract thought; and adults who can more easily manipulate ideas. In addition, different personality patterns mean that some adults will find it easier to learn through their senses than in the abstract. Our increasing knowledge of the organisation of the human brain tells us that the right hemisphere is concerned with emotion, the left with words and speech. One side is usually dominant, which explains why some of us are more emotion-ally/spatially oriented in our perception, others more verbal/analytical. The former tend to use their feelings to help them handle information and can respond particularly well to stories. They will also appreciate visual patterns and dia-grams. The latter make greater use of their powers of reason-ing and rely heavily on words. Information like this helps us appreciate why people reacted differently to the rigid teaching methods of the past. For instance, rote learning was obviously ideal for some but unhelpful for others.

So our task is more complicated than just balancing the needs of children and adults. Adults may range in age from eighteen to eighty-eight or more, and represent many differ-ent subcultures. Some will be open and questioning, others bigoted and inflexible. Some may have theological training, others no Christian knowledge whatsoever. Some who are normally at home in the area of logical thought have got into the habit of switching off their reasoning power on entering church. Intellectual competency, previous experience and preferences, emotional state and spiritual maturity all affect how much we absorb and what we do with it. Some speakers feel constrained to limit the content of what is presented to children, believing the ability to handle abstract concepts sig-nals the point at which formal instruction should begin. How-ever, although we will obviously be selective, children are unlikely to be harmed by a slightly rich spiritual diet, for they can experience quite profound spiritual truths long before they can articulate them. We all manage to enjoy things we do not understand!

All this makes our teaching task seem even more compli-cated! Any one talk can be like a menu with enough choice for everyone to find their special diet, but not so much choice that they never even start to eat. Trying to hear God in a sermon which consists of twenty-five good ideas strung together is like a group of toddlers at a running buffet, overloading their plates with things they cannot digest and dropping most of them immediately! A better picture is that of a well-planned four-course meal. Everybody shares the same starter; the main course is accompanied by a choice from many vegetables; the sweets come in large and small helpings. Everybody says they have had the same menu, everyone starts and finishes each course together: everybody has been fed, though what has been consumed varies enormously!

What themes are suitable?

All-age talks are harder to prepare than adult sermons and ideally a speaker will have both good theological knowledge and communication skills. Both can be learnt, and it is right to encourage those who begin to show gifts in this area to seek further training. Good resource material, such as Scripture Union's *SALT programme*, can help those who are testing out their teaching and preaching skills as well as those who are experienced speakers. It can also help in the planning of a teaching syllabus, so that over a period of time a congregation has a balanced understanding of Christian themes, not just easy or favourite subjects, and has explored all kinds of Bible literature, not just narrative. This kind of help is valuable because it is not only the immediately obvious subjects which are appropriate for all-age learning. For example, children who have known what it is to have pets or even relatives die can find a lot to help them in a talk which mentions death and resurrection, but the dramatic obedience which led Abraham to the brink of sacrificing his child is terrifyingly bewildering even though it lends itself to bloodcurdling and memorable storytelling. Following a carefully planned syllabus also means that a series being followed by children's groups can be added to, not interrupted, by an occasional all-age service – adults being far more capable of carrying forward information over more than one week.

Even if they are familiar, Bible passages need to be read and re-read and preferably slept on for several nights! We may need reference books to help us tease out what the passage meant when it was first written and means in its context; mental effort as we discern what impact the passing of centuries has had on its relevance today; prayer as we decide what aspects are appropriate for this particular congregation at this particular time. Some subjects are unsuitable even for adult sermons, because they cannot be dealt with at the necessary depth in a short time and need to be explored in other ways. Preaching is about glorifying God, proclaiming truth and encouraging people in the Christian life, not about arguing controversial subjects.

One of the major tasks is to help both children and adults handle Scripture. We teach this implicitly by our attitude to the Bible, as well as explicitly by our comments about its content. Hopefully we will speak of it with both reverence and enthusiasm. We will give personal examples both of how the Bible has spoken simply and directly to us, and of where we have struggled to discover its relevance. Though much of what we say will soon be forgotten, our determination to make the Bible work for us today will be obvious to our listeners and may encourage them to develop the same attitude themselves.

Ideas about biblical interpretations have developed considerably in this century and if we are to have credibility we cannot afford to be defensive about this. The Bible contains many different kinds of writings and the story of how they came together and began to be seen as God's word is very complicated. The Christian teaching in the New Testament was by and for people with a totally different world-view from ours. If we have a high view of Scripture we will take as much care in an intergenerational context as in an adult one to discover just how and why a particular passage says what it does. This might involve hard thinking and occasionally we might come to different conclusions from those we have heard in sermons ourselves.

A carelessly literal interpretation in an all-age talk can sometimes do the very thing it is trying to avoid by obscuring the message and thus limiting the power of Scripture. For instance, we need to take particular care over references to prehistory such as those found in the first chapters of Genesis. A preoccupation with scientific detail can distract attention from what the stories are saying about the dependence of the whole created order upon God, the relationship of men and women to creation, and the Jewish teaching about the sabbath. And to give the story of Jonah its true value and thrill, we need to leave people wondering at the forgiveness of God, not wondering whether a man could survive inside a fish if it happened today! We do our children and new adult Christians a disservice if we shield them from the real difficulties in understanding the apparent contradictions and confusions in the Bible. Our aim must be to give individuals the tools to read and interpret the Bible themselves, rather than a list of 'correct answers' to keep with them for ever.

Sometimes we interpret Bible stories literally almost by accident, such as Jesus' parables. From time to time it is worth drawing attention to their purpose with words like: 'Here is a modern version of a story Jesus made up because he wanted his listeners to think about. . .'. Those who have worked with children for many years can also slip into the habit of reading the most obvious message into a passage, or taking the easiest and most colourful approach. For example, to illustrate the story of Noah each generation of children decorates church walls with rows of 'Mr and Mrs Animal'. We all get pleasure from that, but it does not really encapsulate the vital truth the story contains. If the message about evil, judgment and covenant is too difficult for children, perhaps we should leave it for them to encounter later as teenagers and adults; or if we feel justified in keeping the religious zoo at least we should add accompanying words or symbols which say something about God's mercy.

In a congregation which includes people under forty it is likely that adults as well as children may be hearing basic Bible stories for the first time. The 'folk religion' of Britain contains fewer specifically Christian elements than in previous generations, schools teach less about the faith, and even regular church-goers often have only a superficial knowledge of the Bible. From Old Testament times worship has always included the re-telling of the salvation story by groups which include all ages and stages of faith. It seems likely that many Bible stories were meant to be appreciated at different levels at the same time and to mean different things at different times. We need not be surprised or disappointed that some hear only the obvious, others understand the point as it is explained, while some find deeper meanings by themselves.

Stories

It is often helpful to emphasise a Bible narrative by re-telling it, rather than reading it from a translation. Some people dislike Bible stories being embellished. Opinions will always differ about this, but a brief look at some children's religious books and an attentive ear at nativity plays, will show that it happens more often than we realise. Most speakers and preachers 'embroider' the bare bones in the course of story-telling. When this is done thoughtfully it makes the Bible vividly real and exciting, but it is most dangerous when we are unaware of it. The 'fly on the wall' way of telling Bible stories can be very effective. That is, the story is told in the first person; by a key character (Jairus describing the healing of his daughter); by a fictitious character who could have been a witness (Zacchaeus' wife describing how Jesus came for dinner); or by someone quite absurd (the Christmas story from a sheep's point of view). The first of these is commonly used and can stick closely to the Bible text. The last is so obviously fantastic that what has been superimposed on the Bible can be made obvious to all. The middle example is probably the most difficult to handle well because extra details, even if authentic, can change the narrative and distort the original message. So the most startling adaptations of Bible stories are not necessarily the ones to avoid. In a summary or Scripture reading afterwards we can point out what the Bible actually says. Children have less difficulty than adults in alternating between fact and fiction; for instance, in a Christian home there is rarely much confusion between Father Christmas and the characters in the Christmas story. Instinctively they pick up what adults believe to be true.

However, there is much that needs to be said about Christian experience which cannot be gleaned from a single Bible story (try thinking of one, for example, whose principle meaning concerns the Christian's responsibility to oppose the destruction of the environment). In these cases a fictional story is a thoroughly desirable way of teaching – it is, after all, what Jesus did. And even when suitable Bible narratives exist, modern-day stories, whether they are biographies or products of the imagination, supplement them in a way which brings home their relevance. People need to see Christianity 'work' in a context they can understand, even if it is as simple as Basil making peace after a playground fight. Stories work deep in people's emotions, not just in their heads. When they do not ring true they are rightly dismissed, but when they present a simple value by capturing the imagination without the 'threat' that direct teaching carries, they change lives.

Unless a story *is* the message, like a well-told Bible story which can stand by itself, it must not be so overpowering that it outweighs the point it is trying to make. Though we can sometimes make use of children's stories, especially 'folk tales' which do not date, it is important to remember that an all-age congregation will include children whose cognitive development has not reached the stage at which they can appreciate complicated allegory. Even the best-known tales need thorough preparation, and a script can avoid the danger of rambling on too long and ensure that the best possible words are used to express key points.

Stories can help us when their characters think and say things with which we identify. Brief personal anecdotes can be much more powerful than the same points made in a dry analytical way. Modern toys and television characters catch everyone's attention and can be written into our own stories. In one church a series of 'Christian' Mr Men have included Mr Holey, Mr Cross and Mr Red Nosey. Congregations are pleased and flattered when stories are written especially for them, however simple. The Yorkshire village of Woolley heard the lost sheep story in the guise of 'Woolley jumper'; St Andrew's had several visits from the clown 'Stan Drew'. When stories are accompanied by illustrations or mime, a lot is happening simultaneously; things to see, things to hear, deeper messages to think about, and it does not matter if everything is not appreciated by everybody.

Structure

Once we know what we want to say, we can use our imagination to find a framework: three points beginning with P; three points beginning with A, B and C; pictures and diagrams, particularly those which build up gradually. Notice how easily we remember the number 112445778 compared with 427518471, though the digits are the same. We can use repetition and play on words. Often several different approaches are possible, and finding the most appropriate is a struggle, though when we get there we feel it in our bones! It is important to check that a framework is doing its job and is not just worming its way in for the sake of novelty. If we send a congregation home remembering three things, they need to be worth remembering! Some of the best talks sound gimmicky but leave serious points behind in the minds of the hearers. By contrast we have all listened to preaching that sounded serious and sensible but upon reflection turned out to contain very little!

Illustrations

Within structure we need variety so everyone can 'find their own level'. Abstract ideas must be dished up in concrete forms; spiritual concepts illustrated with specifics. The prophets did this brilliantly. To illustrate his preaching Jeremiah used his linen shorts and wine jars (Jeremiah 13:1–14), a visit to the potter (Jeremiah 18:1–6), and a basket of figs (Jeremiah 24:1–10). Amos used locusts, fire and a plumb line (Amos 7:1–9). Jesus also was a 'concrete' preacher and models for us how the most profound ideas can be expressed in imaginative ways, 'salt and light' (Matthew 5:13) or the 'bread of life' (John 6). His parables compared abstract spiritual truths with things in the real world; house building (Matthew 7:24–27) and shepherding (Luke 15:1–7; John 10:1–16) and he often left his listeners to apply the truths for themselves (Mark 4:9).

When visiting Athens, though disturbed by the many idols, Paul was quickwitted enough to hook his Gospel message on to a local story of the 'unknown God' (Acts 17:16–25). Perhaps some ideas around today are like that 'unknown God', open to misinterpretation, yet just waiting to be given some Christian interpretation. Sometimes we may have to take this sort of risk in being very positive about things which others are avoiding, often projecting the darker side of themselves on to what is new or unknown. The media gives us a multitude of ideas on which, like Paul in Athens, to hang old truths.

The child will not automatically translate concrete ideas to the level of abstract thought, but this does not matter. Abstract concepts, such as God's love, are often grasped intuitively by the young, as by the mentally retarded. Good visual aids carry along those who cannot understand. Some points may be heard by adults and older children while younger ones just enjoy the story. Repetitive language or humour brings back those with wandering thoughts. The 'message' can be repeated and reinforced with stories, puzzles, questions, pictures, drama, movement, songs. Several snappy illustrations, drawn from both the child and the adult world, are better than one long rambling story. For instance, a talk about 'Who is my neighbour?' could have a short example drawn from a current situation in world politics, understood only by adults but with names recognisable to many children, and then a brief story about two children at playgroup or school. There is nothing wrong with signposting this by announcing, 'I want to say something to the adults . . . and now here is something I want to say to the boys and girls'. The 'last word' of a talk needs careful planning and some say it should not be an illustration but a firm declaration of the 'message'. We can occasionally finish a talk with a question, or leave it open-ended so that the congregation go away thinking for themselves.

Seeing and doing

Remember the old proverb: 'Hear and forget; see and remember; do and understand'. *Seeing* and *doing* should always be on our checklist when preparing all-age teaching. Pictures and summaries and diagrams are best written large on an overhead projector or an A1 flip chart placed in a prominent position.

Four ways to help people see visual aids
- Invest in proper equipment.
- Simplify as much as possible.
- Use vivid colours.
- Print words larger than seems natural and don't use capitals.

Four things to beware
- The large sheet of paper that keeps falling down.
- The elaborate working model that does not.
- Things which take hours to prepare but only last a moment.
- Items which look huge at home but 'shrink' in church.

Seeing can be combined with doing. For instance, words and pictures can be held in the air, messages scattered around the congregation, strange parcels discovered under chairs. More ways of encouraging the congregation to participate have been outlined in chapter 4. The less sophisticated ways are often the most effective. For instance, a row of children and adults waving things around at the front is more gripping than the same illustration tastefully presented but hanging inanimately on the wall. A Mothering Sunday talk based round the letters of 'MOTHER' used volunteers to hold up letters. Codes on the back allowed them to be re-arranged to reveal the words HOME, ME and MORE, each of which was used as a 'hanger' for serious points. We can collect items from the congregation, perform simple scientific experiments or get people to 'dress up' simply with hats or masks or single items of clothing.

It is important for the speaker to be seen and heard. A raised position helps, but preferably not too far away. Speakers who like to walk about, perhaps even wandering into the congregation, must take care they do not favour one particular section. Some are good at 'dialogue' sermons and we can all cultivate a question-and-answer technique, though it needs courage to begin. The congregation can be encouraged to join in by talking to their neighbour for a minute or two before sharing their ideas. This is particularly important when children are present, for even in all-age worship the different generations do no always interact in the way described in chapter 3. People often say, 'Children have so much to teach us', yet rarely put themselves in a position to prove their point! To ask, 'What do we call the day when Jesus returned to heaven?' involves only one person in answering – probably a child because adults will be too embarrassed to reply – and probably a child with substantial Bible knowledge, so outsiders will feel excluded! However, to say, 'How do you think the disciples felt after Jesus ascended to heaven? Turn to those near you and make a list of suggestions', has a far more valuable impact. Everyone who wishes will be involved, children and adults will have their opinions respected on equal terms, no-one will get the answer 'wrong', the feelings involved in this real story of real people can be compared with our own experience, and there is plenty of opportunity for people to be surprised by ideas they would not have thought of by themselves.

We must also watch our vocabulary, for some words date very quickly. What one generation called gramophones, the next called record players. Do we know the current word – stereos, hi-fi's, stack systems, or is it already something else? If we miss such changes we are failing to hear what is going on in society, a much more serious offence than the neglect of good English! Last year's slang is particularly likely to make teenagers cringe and whisper, 'Irrelevant!' The church still lags behind the rest of society in the area of inclusive language. It is no use protesting that the word 'man' means 'mankind' because in most people's understanding it simply does not! In fact there is much Christian jargon which non-regulars will not understand. The best speakers are those who talk about complicated doctrines in very simple language.

Our tone of voice matters, too. Do we sound as if we are enjoying ourselves and passionately mean what we say? Do we speak loud enough? Do we avoid the equal and opposite dangers of sounding patronising as if our listeners are far beneath us, or pompous as if we are delivering an erudite theological lecture? We should not be talking 'down' to people or above their heads, but addressing them 'straight' as equals. St Francis is reputed to have said, 'Go and proclaim the goods news – and if necessary use words.' We might add to that: 'Watch your language'.

6
USING THE BIBLE

When the Jews returned from exile in Babylon it took several months for the people to organise themselves and set up their civic and political structures. When they had done so they felt the need to mark what they, with God's help, had achieved, so they asked their leaders to arrange a Scripture-reading festival, something which would have been unthinkable in Babylon. A huge, open-air, all-age service was arranged. Because it was not a Temple service, women and children were allowed to gather alongside the men, although separate arrangements were made for children who were too young to understand what was going on.

This was, for them, a journey into unknown territory, for the edited version of the Law (which we now have as the first five books of the Old Testament) was probably only completed during the exile. They were both excited and awed by the prospect. They prepared themselves by praising God in a most fervent and humble way, and then they stood out of respect for what they were about to hear. They were clearly fascinated by what they heard, for it held their attention for several hours (yes, hours!) This is all the more surprising since they were listening to it in a foreign language (during exile they had adopted Aramaic as their day-to-day language, but the Law was in Hebrew). Understandably, they needed help to work out the implications of this thrilling but inaccessible book for their lives, so a group of religious leaders undertook to translate and explain it to them. When the people realised what they had been missing during all those scores of years in exile, their reaction was so intense that even the leaders were taken by surprise. The entire crowd were moved to tears – quite the reverse of the exhilaration that was expected. Of course, there was nothing inappropriate about realising and repenting of their revealed shortcomings, but joy was appropriate too on a holy day. So the religious leaders made a point of comforting and encouraging the congregation, then made sure that a party atmosphere developed. The service led seamlessly into a feast, although unlike many parties, it was notable for its sharing and lack of selfishness.

You can read about the festival in Nehemiah 8:1–12. It is an account which can only lead us to lament that the Bible rarely provokes such intense excitement when it is read publicly today. Of course, the circumstances are different. To start with, the element of surprise has gone. For many, the idea of hearing the Bible read is familiar to the point of boredom (at least, it is perceived like that – in fact it is still possible to shock a congregation by choosing an obscure passage!) However, there are some features of the Bible-reading festival which are pointers to possible ways of intensifying attention to a public reading of Scripture today. To start with, there was a desire to bring together as many ages as possible to hear God's word (but a realisation that those too young to take part were better served by separate arrangements). Second, the reading took place in a context of praise to God and respect for Scripture. Third, it was realised that a bald reading of the text would not bring its whole impact home, so additional help was given to make the reading both understandable and relevant. And last, it was not just a cerebral activity – the full emotional range of tears and joy was let loose. Whatever else this Bible reading was, it most certainly was not dull!

Rediscovering the surprise!

Some recommendations about maximising the impact of the Bible in a service apply to all kinds of congregations, not just an all-age one – for example, selecting with care those who are to read and giving them training in how to present a passage. Suggest how to vary the volume – loud when Goliath is full of scorn, quiet when Saul reacts with dismay. Show when to vary the speed – fast when the storm is in full fury, slow when Jesus speaks the words which calm it. These are the basic requirements for a sensitive reading; if someone feels that he cannot use his voice in this way to vary a monotone, it is wise to look for a different sphere of service in the church where his true gifts can be exercised.

For a very gifted reader, encouragement to inject drama into the voice is all that is required to bring out the excitement of a passage. However, very gifted readers are few and far between. There are other ways to engage attention and some of them are very simple. One way of doubling the impact of a Bible reading is to use two readers. In a gospel account, ask one to speak the words of Jesus and the other to read everything else. The effect of this on, say, the story of the rich young man who went away disappointed from Jesus (Matthew 19:16–26), is to underline the significance of Jesus' words and highlight the tragedy that his challenge was declined. An easy way to arrange a reading in this way is to ask a married couple to prepare – this means they can rehearse without having to leave home. It is so simple to organise that it is astonishing that it is not a regular feature of public readings. If the couple are inexperienced, photocopy the Bible passage and use a highlighter pen to show them who reads what (a small amount of photocopying for this kind of short-term use is not a copyright infringement). If they have had more experience, suggest that they omit little pieces of linking narrative such as 'He said', so that part of the account reads like a dialogue. *The Dramatised Bible* is a rich resource for this kind of presentation (Marshall Pickering).

Other parts of the Bible lend themselves to this treatment as well. For example, the reassuring words of Ecclesiastes 3:1–8 can simply be arranged so that the pairs of contrasting emotions which fit in God's plan are read by two different people. ('A time to weep . . . and a time to laugh . . . a time to mourn . . . and a time to dance'.) In this way the poetic nature of the writing is communicated to the congregation, even if they cannot see it written down. By taking a single step further toward complexity, a reading of Revelation 4 can be made vivid by inviting the congregation as a whole to join in the words of the angels in verses 8 and 11. These can be written on an overhead projector acetate or notice sheet or, if everyone has the same version of the Bible provided for them, invite them to say the phrases which are laid out as poetry.

Obviously, an all-age service offers the opportunity for children to be involved in reading the Bible aloud. It is important to remember, though, that the primary objective is to *communicate* the Bible reading to the children present (as well as the adults); to *involve* the children in the reading is a secondary objective. To hear a child struggle and stammer through a passage which is beyond his or her capacity to understand or pronounce is painful, diminishes the child, and prevents God's word from being declared with clarity. Encouragement and rehearsal can, of course, enable children to contribute very effectively to this part of a service, but it is wise to be cautious when choosing who will lead this important act of worship.

Seeing the Bible

An artist in the congregation can greatly enhance a reading. Because an overhead projector produces an image large enough for a thousand people to see but equally effective for a dozen, it is the best medium for the artist to work with, day or night.

However, not every congregation contains an artist! There are still many overhead projector options open. To accompany a well-known Bible story, images can simply be traced from an illustrated Bible or book of children's stories on to acetate. As a variation, cut the pictures from the pages of the book and place them directly on the deck of the projector in order to create silhouettes. Neither of these requires skill or an application to the copyright holders. It is also possible to have pictures of photographs transferred directly on to acetate using any standard photocopier. This can produce excellent results, but with some drawbacks – the image is black and white (colour can be reproduced by a high street copy shop, but only at considerable expense), special acetates are required (they are coarser than standard ones), and permission is required from the copyright holders unless it is already given at the front of the book. If plenty of preparation time is available, the children of a particular family could be invited to draw pictures of the various stages of the story – an act of service very much in the spirit of 1 Corinthians 14:26 ('When you meet for worship, one person has a hymn, another a teaching, another a revelation from God . . .') and usually both helpful and charming for the congregation. Not only narrative passages can be illustrated in this way – a reading of Psalm 104 could, for example, be accompanied by a series of acetates, some of which are drawn by children and others transferred on to acetate from the holiday photographs of their parents.

Another way to increase understanding of a Bible reading and, at the same time, bring parts of it clearly into focus, is to accompany the reading with simple mime. By this stage, of course, the level of organisational complexity has increased and firm direction and rehearsal are both required. Although, traditionally, children have been used to act out Bible stories (for instance, in a nativity play) there are good reasons to look for alternatives. Although children can be a joy to watch, preparing them to contribute in this way is time-consuming and often fraught with anxiety, especially if they are self-conscious or unwilling. By contrast, adults can perform more complicated actions which have a clear teaching function from which both adults and children can learn.

Advice on the range of possibilities for using drama in a service is given in chapter 8 but here are two examples of how the Bible text itself can be illuminated by simple mime. First a way of underlining the meaning of Luke 21:1–4, the story of the widow's offering, which five children could prepare, to be performed while an adult or teenager reads. The actors are still while the words are read; the reader is silent during the movements:

Jesus looked round (*a child ('Jesus') crosses the front of the room, passing another child who stands holding an offertory bag*) and saw rich men dropping their gifts into the temple treasury (*a third child stands beside the offertory bag preparing to push a wad of notes into it, and poses while a fourth dashes in and takes a photograph of the event with a flash camera, as if for a press release*). He also saw a very poor widow dropping in two little silver coins (*the last child (the 'widow') slips shyly in and drops money into the bag unobtrusively*). He said, 'I tell you that this poor widow put in more than all the others.' (*The 'widow' moves away but stumbles as she passes 'Jesus', who reaches out to steady her and smiles at her as she catches his eye.*) 'For the others offered their gifts from what they had to spare of their riches; but she, poor as she is, gave all she had to live on.'

This simple mime has added several things to the reading – a new interest in a familiar story, an immediate suggestion that the story has a modern relevance (and no fancy-dress costumes to bother with), a visual explanation of the hypocrisy of the rich temple-goers which Jesus condemns in the previous three verses, and a representation of the love and care Jesus had for the poor. None of these could be achieved so clearly by a straightforward reading of the passage, and all of them could be developed as teaching-points in a talk.

The second example could probably not be attempted by children, but their understanding of the relevance of a slightly obscure passage would be enhanced by watching teenagers or adults perform it. Since it is more difficult to get a group of adults together to rehearse, it has been devised for just two, plus a reader. It is part of the Sermon on the Mount and comes from Matthew 5:38–44.

You have heard that it was said, 'An eye for an eye,' (*A pushes B, B pushes A*), 'and a tooth for a tooth', (*A kicks B, B kicks A*). But now I tell you (*both stand still and listen*): do not take revenge on someone who wrongs you. If anyone slaps you on the right cheek (*A hits B on one cheek*), let him slap your left cheek, too (*then on the other*). And if someone takes you to court to sue you for your shirt (*B rips a jacket off A*), let him have your coat as well (*A patiently takes off his sweater and gives that to B too*) and if one of the occupation troops forces you to carry his pack one kilometre (*A motions B to carry these 'heavy' clothes across the room*), carry it two kilometres (*B staggers back with them as well*). When someone asks you for something, give it to him (*B gives A the sweater*); when someone wants to borrow something, lend it to him (*B gives A the jacket*). You have heard that it was said, 'Love your friends, hate your enemies' (*B grabs one end of the clothes and they tussle over them*). But now I tell you (*both stand still and listen*): love your enemies (*they put down the clothes and shake hands*), and pray for those who persecute you (*they adopt a posture of prayer*).

Involving everyone

Some congregations respond with enthusiasm to the way the Bible comes to life when visual stimuli are added to it; others need repeated positive experiences of it before they are convinced that it enhances their understanding. Both need to find their brains and their emotions actively involved in the Bible. The latter group, for instance, could be asked to stand whenever a passage from one of the gospels is read – point out that this act of respect for the words and character of Jesus is a direct link back to Nehemiah's Bible festival and subsequent synagogue worship. The former group might be encouraged to take their own active part in the reading of the Bible. For instance, during the narrative of the visit of the magi to young

Jesus (Matthew 2:1–11), the congregation could be asked to improvise the actions of the magi as the reader recounts the story. A group should lead the actions from the front, with both adults and children copying them in their rows – standing dignified in their Eastern homes, tired as they labour on their long journey, encouraged when they see the star, humble when they enter the house, kneeling in awed worship as the reading finishes.

Equally engaging but, unlike the last example, only accessible to those who are literate, is a reading of the Bible which requires the congregation to consider and respond to the words of, for example, part of an epistle. This example, which would need to be reproduced in some form, is based directly on 1 Thessalonians 5:13–17.

Leader: Be at peace among yourselves.
All: We will be at peace among ourselves.
Leader: Encourage the timid and weak.
All: We will encourage the timid and weak.
Leader: Be patient with everyone.
All: We will be patient with everyone.
Leader: Respond to wrong by doing what is right.
All: We will respond to wrong by doing what is right.
Leader: Make it your aim to do good to all people.
All: We will make it our aim to do good to all people.
Leader: Be joyful and thankful at all times.
All: We will be joyful and thankful at all times.
Leader: The grace of our Lord Jesus Christ be with you.
All: And also with you.

In addition to this, there are many ways of using the Bible interactively in worship. The psalms offer themselves particularly as vehicles for giving God praise. By using them at all-age worship, adults who have been coming to church for many years have a recognisable and scriptural link with the worship that has been precious to them in the past, and children come into contact with an inexhaustible three-thousand-year-old tradition. Psalm 136 is one of those which has always been used interactively – adults and children (even those who cannot read) respond to a worship leader with the repeated line, 'His love goes on forever', a rhythmic and deeply reassuring affirmation that gathers power as it recurs. There are many examples of this use of the Bible in the resource section of this book.

A word of caution

The Bible is a towering book! It was written 'so that you might believe that Jesus is the Messiah, the Son of God' (John 20:31). It was not written as a book of entertainment; it was written as a book of faith. Nothing that has been suggested in this chapter is offered in the hope that children will find the Bible 'fun'. Everything is offered in the serious hope that adults and children together will find an immensely complicated book more engaging to use as a way of hearing God speak. . . . All right, more enjoyable too – but that is a secondary feature!

Every time the Bible is used in all-age worship, we need to ask this: 'How, in our visually-oriented society with its tiny concentration span, can the urgency of this passage come over unmistakably and unforgettably?' Some of our first and most glittering ideas we will reject because, although they are attention-grabbing, the packaging detracts from the content. However, when pictures, movements and explanation all come together to enhance the use of the Bible in worship on a Sunday morning, we will be able to sit down to lunch knowing, as Nehemiah did, that 'the people went home and ate and drank joyfully . . . because they understood what had been read to them.'

7
PRAYER, PRAISE
AND MUSIC

So tell us how you would cope with this situation! You are leading a series of short songs and, to help you establish the right tone, you have invited any children who so wish to join you at the front. The first song has resounded to the praise of God, having all the qualities that make all-age worship special – it was simple, but not childish; you gave a visual focus by asking the children to join you and lead some clapping; and you demonstrated a simple action during the refrain to allow even non-readers to participate actively. Just as you are about to introduce the next song, your three-year-old niece (or daughter, or neighbour – when it actually took place it was a goddaughter) pulls your sleeve to get your attention. You bend down to listen, anticipating that she might say something which can be repeated to inspire the congregation to praise. In fact she pipes into your ear, and thus into the microphone, 'I've got no pants on today'. The guffaw of laughter covers the fact that she has rendered you speechless. You look down at the order of the service to see what song you must announce next. It is a spring-loaded praise number called 'Jump up and down, sing hosanna'. All of a sudden the actions do not seem such a good idea as they did two minutes before!

Balance and participation

There is something absurdly appropriate about the way the girl's innocent spontaneity knocked the poise out of the leader of the service. The truth is that worship requires us to suspend our human dignity together in order to acknowledge God's sovereignty. As a mark of that, Daniel prostrated himself nose-to-earth (Daniel 8:17), Paul shaved his head (Acts 18:18), the Temple builders overflowed with such noisy emotion that those at a distance were not sure whether the din was weeping or laughter (Ezra 3:13), female worshippers in Corinth hid their beautiful hair (1 Corinthians 11:13–16) and David stripped off and danced with all his might (2 Samuel 6:14). Children, for whom active participation in life is more important than dignity, often bring with them to church a greater freedom to use the whole range of emotion, voice and movement – it is not only part of their exuberance, it is part of their humility.

The self-denying sincerity of David's worship was a great problem for one of his wives. Michal, watching from a window, was appalled that her husband, king of the united kingdoms of Israel and Judah, should make such a spectacle of himself in worship (2 Samuel 6:16). However, David insisted that his fervency was not for the benefit of his wife, his servants or his people – he was dancing for the Lord (6:21). Michal's complaint, with which we might have wanted to sympathise had it not been badly motivated and insensitively expressed, has its echoes in those who today refuse to attend an all-age service because of the damage they fear it will do to the dignity of public worship. To see others humbling themselves before God can be an embarrassing sight – *but worship is for participants, not spectators*. Children seem to have an inbuilt understanding of the appropriateness of lively, serious, participative worship. Those who take offence need to ask themselves why.

In the balance of joy and abandonment, reverence and care which features in David's worship, we may find pointers to help our own praise thirty centuries later!

Music

The second book of Samuel shows us a wonderfully uncompromising scene on the occasion when the Covenant Box was taken into Jerusalem: 'David and the whole house of Israel were celebrating with all their might before the Lord, with songs and with harps, lyres, tambourines, sistrums and cymbals' (6:5). It is not clear whether the music they played suited everyone's taste, but it is plain that there was nothing half-hearted about it.

Those who seek a musical expression of praise which is suitable for today's culture have to face the fact that there is no single musical culture shared across the generations and groupings. We are a society in which everyone's chosen style of music is pumped personally into his or her ears from an individual plastic box, leaving the rest of us to guess from the relentless *tish-ti-tish-ti-tish* of the graphically equalised bass what it is of which we are hearing so little, and yet so very much too much! For those seeking a means by which a congregation of many ages and demographic groups can bring their musical praise to God in an all-pleasing way, there are perhaps two facts to realise before anything else. One – this is impossible. Two – that is no reason for failing to try!

Obviously many congregations do fail to try. They gather around them a group of like-minded people and expect anyone who has different tastes either to endure patiently or to find a home elsewhere (and that applies as much to those who refuse to believe that the Holy Spirit can have inspired any music written since the War as it does to those who refuse to attempt anything that cannot be sung to three guitar chords). Very often churches of this kind find themselves wondering why young families leave the congregation, or frustrated that the absence of anyone elderly deprives them of the mature voices of wisdom that would encourage them during difficult times, or guilty that teenagers would rather stand on the street corners looking bored than cross the door-step. A truly all-age congregation must try to cater for an impossibly wide range of needs. Those who watch the world changing with alarming acceleration and wonder where they belong in it need to be able to go to church and recognise fixed points on which they can depend – songs that link them firmly to the assurance they had when they first believed, and an orderliness which they can understand and have confidence in, markedly in contrast to the turmoil which dictates most of their lives. And those who need to be stimulated and challenged because so many of the world's experiences are boring or fleeting need to be able to go to church with a sense of open expectancy about what the Spirit may astonish and excite them with that day. Paradoxically, a church will always be a hospital and a battle-field at one and the same time!

If they are carefully chosen and well presented, many 'traditional' hymns can take their place in all-age worship.

Careful choice and presentation, however, means more than allowing the course of time to honour particular favourites. It means. . . .

• Selecting versions of hymns that have replaced 'thou' and 'ye' with 'you'. This rarely damages anything about a song except its sentimental appeal.

• Omitting verses if they are untrue ('Not a doubt or a fear, not a sigh nor a tear, can abide while we trust and obey'), obscure ('O generous love, that he who smote in man for man the foe, the double agony in man for man should undergo' – guesses on a postcard to Cardinal Newman, care of 'Praise to the holiest in the height'), or simply too numerous.

• Favouring hymns which have simple refrains, and then pointing out to children that even if they cannot manage all the words there is a part specially for them to join in, such as 'Jesus Christ is risen today, Alleluia!' or the more recent 'Make way! Make way!'

• Choosing hymns in which the overall thrust of what is being addressed to God is clear, even if not everyone will understand the subtleties, and introducing it in such a way that both children and adults are clear what the song is about. (Perhaps 'Crown him with many crowns' is a good example of a song which contains imagery that is rich, but can be explained with a single, well-planned sentence of introduction.)

• Deciding occasionally that it is of such value to sing an exclusively adult masterpiece such as 'Immortal, invisible God, only wise' or, 'Led like a lamb to the slaughter' that you will do it without apology, meanwhile giving children something different to do as their act of praise to God – perhaps drawing something which they particularly want to thank God for and preparing to show what they have drawn to the rest of the congregation when the singing is over. In this way children will hear the music and words of hymns which will one day mean a great deal to them, but without having to tackle their complexity before they are able.

• Providing a careful balance between complex hymns of many verses and short, simple, immediately accessible songs.

It is very often helpful to begin an all-age service with a substantial hymn of this kind, be it ancient or modern, since this gives a strong beginning to the act of worship and sets what is to follow in the context of words with theological depth and objectivity. This does not prevent a musician or group of singers playing instrumental music or singing songs in praise of God before the 'official' beginning of a service – indeed, for the congregation to arrive to the calming, mind-centring (new-tune-teaching?) sound of worshipful music can be particularly beneficial at an all-age service when children and the adults who have brought them often need to change down a gear before they are ready to come into God's direct presence. And of course, a few words of welcome addressed to both adults and children can preface the opening hymn in such a way that all have the expectation that the service will be relevant to them.

Just as it is possible to choose traditionally adult hymns which will be accessible to children, so it is possible to choose children's songs which are appropriate for adults. The object is not to offer worship which is trivial, but worship which is simple – there is a profound difference! 'Wide, wide as the ocean' is a good song. It is old, yes! It was written for children, yes! It has actions associated with it, yes! But it is a good song about a powerful truth, and if adults cannot find value in singing it they must ask themselves why! In the eighty years since it was written, a huge number of songs have been composed which address God with the simplicity that is required for both adults and children to share them.

It is just as important to be discriminating when choosing and presenting these songs as it is when choosing more substantial ones. . . .

● Announce them in a way which shows that your expectation is that adults will join in as well as children. If there are actions, make sure that all the adults who are leading the service at the front of the room demonstrate them so that everyone, regardless of age, has confidence that it is correct to join in. Having done that, make sure that no one is pressurised in any way to do or sing something which makes them feel uncomfortable.

● Avoid songs in which the 'fun' content so obviously exceeds the 'praise' content that discriminating worshippers feel they are being required to come before God with trivia.

● In songs with a pronounced rhythm, encourage clapping so that children too young to read will feel able to participate in a genuine way. It is best, however, to encourage clapping by example, rather than by instruction, with the lead given by the band, choir, singers, minister or whoever else is in a leadership role at that service.

● Vary rhythmic songs with reflective songs, so that the congregation experiences the whole range of approaches to God.

• Explain difficult words such as 'Alleluia' and 'Hosanna' over and over again.

• Introduce these songs with the same seriousness that you introduce traditional hymns, so that the congregation is more aware of the continuity of the praise than the difference of the style.

• There is no need to feel that every line of every song must have an action with it. If the words have a simple directness, then that is often powerful enough by itself to allow both children and adults into God's presence with praise.

• Clearly announce what is happening before each song – a series of songs which appear unannounced as overhead projector images can be helpful in allowing adult praise to flow, but for children and for the elderly, this can be harmfully bewildering.

• If the structure of the service allows it, there is much to be said for having a group of these kind of songs early in a service, and following it later with a group of songs which are more developed theologically and musically (either when children have left to meet in their peer groups, or presented in such a way that they still feel part of the service even if they can only listen to the music). Of course, some equally effective structures require this to take place the other way round.

• Percussion instruments, especially home-made ones, allow children too young to read to take a full part in praising God. If this has been introduced sensitively, most young children are able to sense remarkably well whether or not percussion is appropriate for a particular song and can be left to make their own judgments about when to play – although an example to follow at the front of the room is very helpful, too.

It is impossible to undervalue times when children and adults are singing praise to God side by side. From a child's point of view, it provides a model of wholehearted, mature response to God in corporate worship. It previews the heritage of praise into which we hope children will grow. From an adult's point of view, it releases the ability to offer not just voices and intellects but bodies and emotions in praise of God. For children there will be other opportunities in church life to sing the rhymes and fun songs which are appropriate only for them – perhaps in regular children's groups. For adults there will be other opportunities in church life to sing the densely metaphored, musically complex songs, chants and anthems whose richness is important to their spirituality – perhaps at an evening service or meeting of a home group.

But to praise God together is special! When he sees the people he loves dropping their personal preferences in order to make a joyful noise to him, the Lord must surely rejoice!

Quiet

Even a king gets excited in the presence of the King of kings. However, the exuberance of David's praise was balanced with quiet, reflective prayer. Not only did David dance joyfully before the Covenant Box, he also went and sat down in front of it to contemplate the greatness of God, to reflect on the questions the Lord had left unanswered, and to open himself to God's blessing (2 Samuel 7:18–29). In just the same way and for just the same reasons it is important that an all-age service has its periods of stillness and silence.

Times of quiet, though, need for practical reasons to be presented in a different way when children and babies are in the congregation as well as adults. Children, and indeed some adults, need clear direction as to how to use the silence, so that it is not merely an awkward pause. For example, suggestions for what to think or pray about during the silence are very helpful, especially with guidance about ways of thinking – should the congregation formulate words, or fill their minds with pictures, or prayerfully imagine the needs of particular people, or dream up the sounds and smells of a Bible story? Something to look at and reflect on silently is a positive help as well – an illustration on an overhead projector, a stained glass window, a Christian symbol such as a cross, even the uniquely created pattern of a fingertip. You will find many suggestions for imaginative ways of using quiet in chapter 8 of the resource section of this book.

It goes without saying that with children present times like these need to be shorter than if they are for adults only – but they need be none the less powerful for that. Several short silences, connected by thought-provoking words, are more helpful in an all-age setting than a long meditation. If the person leading worship senses a restlessness after a while, that is an indication that it is time to move on – perhaps to a sensitively chosen musical item.

In theory, babies and very young children should sense the quiet around them and respond by stilling themsleves. In reality, however, there is every possibility that a crawling toddler will choose the most peaceful moment to bump his or her head on a chair. Typically this is followed by a tense hush during which the whole congregation forgets what they were meditating on and awaits the inevitable howl. Because this is bound to happen, the whole tenor of a service needs to suggest that it is not going to matter when it does! This is yet one more reason why a creche or equivalent escape route is always necessary, for the ease of both the distressed child and the embarrassed parent. One way of making everyone feel at home with the presence of children is to announce that when toddlers are making a happy noise they are welcome in the room because however loud their happiness is it is part of the congregation's praise, but that if they are making an unhappy noise no one expects that they must be kept in the room against their will.

Giving, sharing and eating

The vision of God in worship liberated David in his giving to God (2 Samuel 6:17) and his sharing with his fellow-worshippers (6:19). There are no direct equivalents of these actions for today's congregations – neither a financial offering nor a communion service has the same theological meaning as David's sacrifice. However, there are plenty of activities which can offer the same opportunities for joyful fellowship. If presented in an appropriate way a shared meal after a service, in which everyone brings enough food for one and pools it, can be perceived as part of the worship of the church rather than a refreshment tacked on the end. Even just coffee and cold drinks following a service can enrich the life of an all-age church, giving an unpressured chance for newcomers and fringe members to develop relationships and feel at one with established members, for single people to enjoy the company of children, and for those with particular needs to find prayer and support from those who can offer it in a stress-free environment.

As with every other aspect of all-age worship, however, special account must be taken of the fact that many generations are present. Children, for example, have particular needs. A definite but much overlooked one is security – children playing near an open door while their parents are engrossed in conversation are vulnerable. It is good regularly to ask the congregation to cooperate in preventing any physical dangers, and to insist that children tell their parents which adults they are playing with if they are out of their view. Another need that children have is to avoid boredom – particularly so that they grow up with positive images of church life. It is best that times of fellowship such as these are kept to a length that matches the children's patience – if the meal or coffee break is to be lengthy, an organised game for the children while adults talk might transform their enjoyment of it.

But children are not the only ones with special needs at these times. For example, an elderly person may well need a chair, a drink brought to him, someone to talk to, and the assurance that he will not be used as a goalpost by restive teenagers. A congregation which does not notice this automatically might benefit from it being mentioned during a sermon on service or hospitality. Fringe members of the church, for whom it is hard enough to cross one threshold, often find it daunting to have to go to a different room (or even a different building) to get a cup of coffee and may melt away unnoticed. The desirability (and appropriateness) of eating and drinking in the same room in which the congregation has just praised God is great.

Of course, David was generous not only to those who were praising with him, but to God himself. There are many different ways of allowing a church to realise both the blessing and the necessity of giving to the Lord's work. In an all-age context, probably the least helpful is the long-standing practice of passing a bag or plate along the rows. This is usually accompanied by a frantic scrabbling in wallets and handbags to find some loose change which is pressed into a child's hand only seconds before it passes out of sight. This is hardly a good way of teaching children the value of regular, organised, sacrificial giving! In fact, it doesn't teach adults much about giving either and squanders what the tax-man is happy to give to God's work if only he is asked!

However, if most of a church's giving is done directly through covenants and bank orders, there is another potential problem – that children and visitors develop the assumption that somehow a church, its evangelism and its pastoral care operate without any expense. There are several ways of tackling this, and a combination of some of them seems desirable. Firstly, regular teaching about giving can be given both in all-age talks and, in depth, on occasions when only adults are present. Then, even if an offertory is not taken every week, the money which has been given by alternative means can be referred to and dedicated to God (a few suitable prayers are given on page 153 in the resource section). It could be suggested to parents that they include in their children's pocket money or allowance a certain amount which could be set aside for God's work, and then discuss with them the freedom they have to give it to the church, choose another charitable destination, or secretly spend it on sweets! Sharing of toys and games (and, of course, electric drills and hedge trimmers) can be encouraged as a regular part of the church's life, with the saved money released for God to make use of in any way he prompts. And most importantly, children and adults alike can be helped to realise that there are other ways of giving an offering to God even if they have no money of their own. For example, tasks they do to help the smooth running of the church and the creative work they produce in praise of God are all part of their offering (chapter 8 of the resource section of this book has many such ideas). When children realise that their best creative efforts and most costly acts of service are part of their Christian dedication, it is a small step for them to bring their financial decisions under God's control later in life.

Dance and movement

This will mean different things to different people. For some it will bring to mind a group who have choreographed and rehearsed a beautiful sequence of steps to interpret a song or piece of music in praise of God. For some it will remind them of their congregation's openness to let the rhythm of the hymn they are singing dictate what their legs do! For some it will involve following a set of movements which the whole congregation do together to match the words of their song with appropriate actions.

All of these are important because they remind us that worship is what we do with our entire bodies and our whole lives. As surely as being still is a vital ingredient to all-age worship, so is movement.

A rehearsed dance group can be valuable in this way because it brings a control and interpretive precision to movement in a way that spontaneous congregational dance does not. However, it is important that the congregation realises that what they see and hear is not just a performance, it is an act of worship which people have prepared in the way Paul describes in 1 Corinthians 14:26. The creative gifts which God has given them are being shared so as to inspire and strengthen the rest of the congregation. Encourage everyone to understand their enjoyment of what they see as part of their praise. Be careful, however, that this does not become associated exclusively with children's events or special occasions. One church 'always had a dance at Easter' and after a few years the habit was hard to break! Some well-resourced churches have permanent groups on stand-by; others can quickly form an *ad hoc* group when appropriate. When a lengthy item is to be included in the service it needs thorough preparation and planning. However, it is sad when drama or dance become the preserve of experts, or when a church's experience is confined only to one style. Dance need not have the ethereal 'Laura Ashley' look, for it can include robust performances by males as well as females. All ages, including young children, can work together on a simple circle dance or can demonstrate worship-actions to songs.

Congregational movement can be even more valuable in an all-age setting, because it allows even the youngest children to worship God on equal terms with adults. When it comes to reading a psalm aloud, an adult can praise God with greater understanding than a child. But when it comes to clapping hands or moving feet, a child's praise is in every way equal to an adult's. In fact, in the wholeheartedness and freedom with which they do it, children's contributions to the worship of the church may well be superior at this point.

In many churches, action songs led enthusiastically by one or more adults are the most helpful way to give both adults and children initial confidence that their movement is part of their total worship, and that God is pleased with it. Spontaneous movement and dance may follow later, when and if the Spirit leads a congregation to develop its own impetus.

There are also many ways in which movement can aid prayer and enrich praise without any music at all. Christians have accompanied their prayers with actions for centuries without recognising it as such – kneeling or closing their eyes or folding their hands to pray, walking in procession or pilgrimage, lifting their arms in praise, genuflecting, making the sign of the cross in benediction or out of reverence. These have become so familiar in church life that congregations have even developed traditions that dictate which they approve of and which they don't! But new expressions of active praise can help people explore the love or the holiness or the power of God in ways free of past associations – which is why chapter 8 of the resource section is such an important part of this book.

Two things are, of course, vital. First, that children are never required to do things which adults are not – for children acquire faith by example as well as by teaching, and we do not want them to grow out of praising at the same time that they grow out of actions. And second, that a congregation is always invited to move, never required to – so that those unable to join in because of disability, dignity, drowsiness or downright dreariness are allowed to approach God on their own terms and explore the freedom he gives in their own time. In this respect it is particularly important that adolescents find their own level of involvement, even if it means they do not even sing – for some just being there is a considerably costly act, and we need to learn to take as much pleasure at seeing them skulking on the edge of God's people as God himself does!

Prayer

'O Lord Almighty, God of Israel, you have revealed this to your servant . . . so your servant has found courage to offer you this prayer' (2 Samuel 7:27). So said David when the dancing was done, the praise was offered, the sins had been forgiven, and the needs of the kingdom of Israel stretched before him with daunting clarity. He was alone at the time, but on many occasions he led his people in public prayer, much as we will need and want to.

The style of prayer which features at an all-age service is usually dictated by the tradition or the denomination of the congregation. It has to be said, however, that none of the traditions of public worship which dominate the life of our churches was developed with the needs of an intergenerational congregation in mind. In every tradition without exception, those who try to integrate children into adult worship without any change to its style find that the results are unsatisfactory. For example, 'new churches' in which the unstructured worship is open to the leading of the Spirit find that if the invitation to share words and songs of praise, prophecy or tongues is offered in an adult way, only adults feel free to participate – even if the Spirit leads children to contribute freely when they are in their peer groups. In churches which have a written liturgy of some theological depth, there is often a sense among children that this part of the service is not for them – the problem is not necessarily that the language is archaic or that any individual word is beyond their comprehension, but that the clauses are put together with a complexity and length which stretch them beyond the staying power of young minds. And in churches where the liturgy is not a written one, but one tacitly acknowledged by many years of practice, there is frequently a problem that any individual item is so long that even if children wanted to identify with the content of the prayer or make thoughtful use of the silence, they are simply unable to – despite the fact that they may be active participants in times of prayer when they meet in peer groups.

The most difficult hurdle to leap when preparing forms of prayer which are suitable for intergenerational worship is to let go of some things which are precious about adult worship. One of the needs of children is the recognition of an order to what they are experiencing – and that may mean planned activity even in a 'spontaneous' service. Only within these limits can children own an act of worship as relevant to them and be open to the Spirit leading them to participate. Another need is a syntax and vocabulary that children can understand without having achieved a substantial reading age – only when there is a generous slack in the ropes that tie services to the seventeenth century can today's children participate fully, with an openness to God through the help of the Spirit.

So, remembering that God will graciously accept our prayers no matter how well or badly we offer them, what is needed to make public prayer accessible across as many ages as possible? And how can those at home in different traditions adapt what they do to meet those needs?

● **Simplicity**. Not banality, but simplicity! This means replacing religious jargon with straightforward language (for example, changing phrases such as 'Now let's just move into a time when we really bless the Lord' to those which are straightforward to adults and children alike: 'Let us all praise God for his greatness and goodness in a way which will bring joy to him'). It also means restraining the excesses of liturgical language, ('We have followed too much the devices and desires of our own hearts', which despite being a phrase of wonderful sonority, may have to give way to: 'Too often we have done just as we please, knowing that our actions angered you'). It need not mean avoiding all metaphorical language, which would make for earth-bound dreariness, but language which is not concrete needs to be signposted clearly or used in similes, ('We have disobeyed the plans you have for us, like lost sheep who have wandered miles from the path'). In a written liturgy, this can be achieved with thoughtful planning, but when prayer is open for anyone to lead, the cooperation of the whole congregation needs to be obtained by sensitive teaching, good example, and sometimes individual and private conversation about what is appropriate.

● **Poetry**. This is not something which God requires, because the function of the Holy Spirit is to translate our words with unimaginable beauty, power and correctness (Romans 8:26–7). However, humans of all ages need it, because it lifts our awareness that to bring our thanks or intercession to the almighty God is in every way more valuable and serious than a chat with a chum. Children, of course, have an innate feeling for rhyme and rich langauge, but for those who are praying week by week, to compose it is a tall order. When prayer is always open, only experience can lead people to find the colourful midpoint between bland and florid language. When prayers are prepared, it is helpful to write (and then read) the clauses line by line like poetry; to include occasional alliteration ('Lord God, who loves to hear our praise, and longs to answer our prayer. . .'); to rehearse prayers aloud so that they can be edited to give them a recognisable rhythm (the last example serves again), and to punctuate them with a response so that all may echo the prayer as their own (for example, half a dozen short prayers could be interspersed with the leader saying 'Loving Father of us all', to which everyone responds, 'Hear the prayers of your family').

● **Brevity**. In all honesty, this generation's adults, as well as teenagers and children, are better able to make use of several short prayers than one long one.

● **Breadth**. A service that explores the whole spiritual experience of Christian life needs to include elements of confession, praise, thankfulness, prayer for the needs of the world and the congregation, and opportunities for people to commit themselves to God in faith and obedience. These all have a place in traditional liturgies, and they need to be present if a new local liturgy is being developed or if a service has no formal structure.

● **A visual focus**. Although convention and experience have taught us that it is easier to concentrate on our prayers if our eyes are closed, to have something to look at is also an aid to concentration. It allows a generation which is more used to collecting information visually than verbally (and that includes adults as well as children) to form their prayers in the way that has become the most natural method of communication in all other areas of life. With the invention of the overhead projector, the ease with which images can be shown in daylight to large numbers of people has been transformed. From views of beauty which inspire our praise to photographs of the people for whom we are interceding, it is hard to think of any kind of prayer which could not be enhanced by the occasional use of pictures and visual symbols. The creativity which God has breathed through us should also prompt us to use our ability to make and enjoy beautiful or meaningful things in the context of prayer. Chapter 8 of the resource section of this book suggests many ways in which simple congregational artwork, undertaken where people sit and without messy equipment, can set free their desire to pray and to praise God in a reverent way which words alone might not achieve.

● **Appropriate language**. While simplicity is important, it must not lead to language which is childish. At an all-age service it is just as inappropriate to pray that God will help us to play nicely with our toys and teddies as it is to pray that God will strengthen us in the face of sexual temptation! Language should not let adults off the hook (confess 'wrong things we have said, thought and done', not 'times we have been naughty'); it should not assume that everyone present lives in a family which consists of children with two parents (it is a rare church indeed where a majority of the congregation is in that category, so prayers thanking God for family life need to be worded with particular sensitivity); it should not assume that everyone is in paid employment (to pray for events 'at home, at work and at school' is a helpful phrase); and even if the congregation is not ready to use feminine words to address the holy God who is so infinitely great beyond human telling that gender is meaningless, it is important to use language which allows us to appreciate in him the qualities we glimpse in a perfect mother as well as in a perfect father.

● **Involvement**. The open and confident involvement of adults in prayer takes time to develop, and the involvement of children and teenagers beside them takes even longer. In churches where informal congregational prayer is the norm, it may be necessary to help children feel the freedom we want them to have to share in this part of the church's worship. It is, to be frank, a mystery why near-identical churches find that in one children participate enthusiastically in prayer or the use of certain spiritual gifts, but in another children feel obliged to leave only adults to contribute. Perhaps churches in the latter category need to do more than issue the invitation to participate to all – they need to discriminate positively to allow children to feel at ease. It can help, for instance, to open such a time of prayer or praise exclusively to children in the first instance, and then to adults as well (this helps children's natural inclination to defer to an adult who has something to say). It is also helpful for the leader to give a clear indication of the kinds of contribution which are expected at that point in the service – for instance, ask the congregation to focus on news or events or items for which they particularly want to thank God. Needless to say, if the leader introduces this over the heads of children using a relentlessly adult vocabulary and tone of voice, he or she should not be surprised that children play no part.

• **Response**. churches which practice a more formal type of worship will also wish to find ways of involving children actively in prayer. For them responsive prayers, in which a phrase is repeated by the congregation over and over again, can be of great value. The repetition is important since it allows even those who cannot read to join in meaningfully. Even very young children pick up a clear, rhythmic phrase as it is repeated during the course of a prayer, and this kind of involvement is very effective indeed. There needs to be a clear indication of where the response comes and this is achieved by the leader saying a short phrase which he or she has already announced to be the cue for the response. A definite rhythm always helps this, and occasionally rhyme and alliteration do as well. The leader's cue should begin with a strong-sounding word, to alert the people in readiness, and the congregation's response should have its main verb or noun as the second or third word (not the first, which is needed to gather all the voices together) or towards the end of the phrase. For example, short statements in praise of God by the leader could be followed by the cue, 'Glory to God in the highest,' with all responding, 'And peace to his people on earth.' The books of the Bible, particularly Psalms, are a ready source of responses such as these.

• **Leadership of all ages**. Some services lend themselves to having intercession prepared and led by a family, each of whom contributes one or more prayers using language which comes naturally to them, young or old. In order to build up the fellowship of the church, it is also possible to put a family together with a single person or older couple to do this. Suggest that they meet for a meal during the week before in order to decide how to approach the task (and to enjoy each others' company in a way which might not happen unprompted).

• **Group prayer**. Either kind of service may lend itself to inviting people to pray in small groups. In order for children and adults to participate fully, they need to be reassured about their physical comfort, so it is wise to specify that they do not need to move their chairs; simply to turn on their seats for a short while so that three or four can hear what each other are saying without raising their voices. As a rider, ask those in familes to look round and see whether anyone who came to church alone would like to join their cluster, but also point out that it is quite acceptable for anyone who prefers to pray silently by themselves to do so. Be clear in your instructions about what you want people to pray for, and whether you want them to begin by discussing their topic for prayer or thanksgiving, or to pray straight away. It is good to indicate how long the groups will have and how they will know that their time is coming to a close (music of some kind is a good way of moving from this kind of prayer to the next event). As always, tell adults that if they are fortunate enough to have children in their group they should respect and take part in their prayers, and tell children that if they are fortunate enough to have adults in their group they should listen carefully as they join in, and ask later about anything they did not understand.

The resource section in the second half of this book is a response to our awareness that many find this part of the life of an intergenerational church the most difficult to develop. It is offered in the hope that in it churches which need more structure will find the order that allows children, teenagers and adults to approach God joyfully, expectantly and reverently. It is offered in the hope that in it churches which need less structure will find the freedom to unlock the creative potential for worship that only the meeting of young and old in the presence of God can make possible. It is offered defiantly in the hope that never again will a child bring a jigsaw to church because he is too bored to realise that the worship going on around him belongs to him. And it is offered humbly in the hope that God will take joy in what he sees and hears.

8
OTHER INGREDIENTS FOR WORSHIP

Why can't we go back to the 'good old days' when worship was planned by the minister and everyone else just went along? Surely that wonderful worship experience described at the beginning of chapter 6, when the Jews rediscovered the Bible on their return from exile, was arranged with a lot less fuss than all-age worship today? The early church managed without overhead projectors and visual aids and quizzes, so why can't we?

Today we live in a world which has changed considerably, even since the days of our grandparents. At school and in adult training we have learnt to expect multi-media presentations. Our entertainment is extremely sophisticated. We take up elaborate hobbies that demand so much maintenance that they are more like a second career. We watch television, which brings a whole world of experiences into the living room, though our appreciation of them is sometimes illusory. In the affluent West we spend huge amounts of time and energy and money on choosing food and clothes and items for our homes and gardens, on presenting them in new ways and keeping them in good order. Though as Christians we may sometimes pretend we have a neutral attitude to all this, the need for novelty is inescapably part of our culture.

Some Christians enthusiastically take on almost any new idea simply because it is new. Others beat a retreat into the safety of a Christian 'ghetto', pursing their lips like Mrs Proudie in *Barchester Towers*, and muttering about not taking on 'the ways of the world'. Our different reactions probably have more to do with our character type than with theology. It is true that Paul warns against conforming to the world's standards but he is writing less about what we *do* than about our *attitude*. In Romans 12:2 he then goes on to say, 'Be transformed by the renewing of your minds, so that you may discern what is the will of God – what is good and acceptable and perfect.' Our task is to try to work out God's attitude. According to the Pharisees' interpretation of the Law, Jesus himself was not particularly careful about what he did and where he went. He ate food prepared without the proper ritual washing (Mark 7:2) and mixed with people who had been labelled as undesirables (Mark 2:16). His attitude to the woman with persistent bleeding illustrates how he challenged the conventional attitude to purity (Mark 5:25–34) and he taught that any contamination comes from what is already going on inside a person, not from what they do (Mark 7:18–23). So at one level we do not have to be too careful about what we experience. However, what we do 'must be a help to the church' (1 Corinthians 14:26b) and not be a stumbling block to the faith of others (Romans 14:21).

In 1 Corinthians 12 and 14 Paul says a lot about worship ingredients. He encouraged the Corinthians to allow the Spirit to work through them in worship in a multitude of ways which would have been unlikely at an earlier time. Such descriptions of spiritual gifts do not give us a definitive list but rather suggests the way the Spirit works creatively. Sometimes it is hard to see where a natural gift ends and the Holy Spirit takes over, and we probably do not even need to try to make the distinction. We could paraphrase Paul as saying that anything *might* happen in worship, but it must happen 'in a proper and orderly way' (1 Corinthians 14:40). This suggest a sensitive blend of spontaneity and planning. Some of the worship 'ingredients' in this chapter were around in Bible times. The way we handle those which were not must be consistent with the spirit of what Jesus and Paul taught.

À la carte or table d'hôte?

In a formal meal the starter is usually followed by the main course, then by the dessert and then by the cheese. Previous chapters have emphasised the importance of continuity and order. As in a meal, people need to know where they are in worship, what is coming next and whether the end is in sight. On the other hand, we would be disappointed if every meal were identical. A conventionally grilled pork chop could be spiced up with a glamorous sauce; some cultures serve cheese before dessert; an extra sorbet might be slipped in for a special occasion. Sometimes, of course, we are healthier with just one course! This chapter is like the one on 'extras' at the end of a cookbook. It includes many things which did not fit elsewhere. Most are not essential; indeed a service with a bit of everything would be impossible to digest! Yet each can add variety and 'spice up' the goings on. If something is done for the first time it will automatically get people's attention. This can be turned to good effect, but if it has not been thought through carefully it will be remembered for all the wrong reasons. New items need to be introduced with confidence, not with apology, and are best used sparingly, for worship is not a variety show. However, the motive for including something can be modest and not obviously 'spiritual'. Brief activities can be used to 'change gear' between two parts of the service, give the opportunity for movement, or keep the attention of the under fives.

Drama

The Old Testament Jews were always acting out the important events of their history, to keep them fresh in the memory and to pass on their story to the next generation. The prophets often portrayed their message by dramatic actions. Ezekiel ate a scroll as a sign that he was taking in God's message and would speak it out again to the people (Ezekiel 3:1–3). Jeremiah put a yoke around his neck to help him explain to the king of Judah how the people would come under the yoke of Babylon (Jeremiah 27:2,12). It does not matter whether the prophets did these things literally or whether they just acted them out when proclaiming their message; each makes the point equally well.

In the Christian era these things have continued to be important. In fact it could be said that, as far as England is concerned, Christians invented drama when the mediaeval mystery plays spilled out of churches onto the streets. Today drama can be both a helpful way to learn and an inspiration to worship. All-age services are ideal for introducing a first taste. Drama is more likely to be 'given a chance' by the cynics in this context, and may later come to be used more extensively in the church.

When drama is used for teaching purposes we need to be

clear about our objectives, and the worship leader will want to have the final say about what fits in with the overall theme. It can be embarrassing to discover at the last minute that a sketch is totally inappropriate, though cooperation in the early stages should prevent this happening. Many excellent books of scripts are available, though these are often so complicated that some churches feel discouraged. If a congregation contains someone who can write tailor-made pieces, all the better! Often the simplest way of presentation is the most effective. For instance, it takes less time to prepare a mime to a script which is read than for people to learn lines. Mime is particularly appropriate for children as the message will be clear from the script even if things go wrong in the actions!

Chapter 6 suggested ways for the congregation to join in Bible readings, but there are other ways of enabling everyone to participate dramatically. Congregational responses can include simple hand movements; cheers, boos and clapping; or speaking phrases displayed on flash cards. The following script, based on two parables from Luke 15, requires only three readers and no preparation. It could be distributed to the whole congregation, and includes parts where non-readers can be encouraged to join in.

Narrator: Once Jesus told two stories to show how much God loves us. If he was telling them today, they might sound like this: There was once a woman who had ten silver coins. They were a wedding present and meant a lot to her.
Woman: My Sid gave these to me the day we was wed. He had them made up into a necklace so that I could always be reminded of how much he thinks of me.
All: Cor, they look nice!
Narrator: Then, one day . . .
All: Clink, clink, gone!
Woman: Help, help, I've lost one of me coins!
Left: Look under the carpet!
Right: Look behind the armchair!
Left: Look in the kitchen!
Right: Look in the bedroom!
Woman: It's no good I can't see. The light's not good enough.
Narrator: It's pretty dusty in there, too!
Left: Get a torch!
Right: Get a broom!
All: (*Make sweeping noises*)

Woman: I've found it! I've found it!

All: Hurrah!

Woman: Come on everyone. Let's have a party. I'd lost my coin and now I've found it.

All: Well done. Now your necklace is complete again. Let's all celebrate!

Narrator: Jesus then told another story: There was once a shepherd who had a hundred sheep.

All: Baa! Baa! Baa!

Narrator: One day he was counting them.

Left: Ten.

Right: Twenty.

Left: Thirty.

Right: Forty.

Left: Fifty.

Right: Sixty.

Left: Seventy.

Right: Eighty.

Left: Ninety. (*Right and Left alternate numbers up to ninety-nine*)

Shepherd: Ninety-nine. I've lost one!

All: Are you sure? Count again.

Shepherd: All right. But you help me.

All: One, two, three (*then 'rhubarb'*).

Shepherd: How many do you make it?

All: You're right. It is only ninety-nine.

Shepherd: I must go and find my lost sheep.

Left: Why bother? You've got ninety-nine. It's only one.

Right: You probably won't find it anyway.

Left: It's its own fault. It shouldn't have wandered off.

Right: Why risk your life for it?

Shepherd: Because it's my sheep. I know its name and it knows my voice. My flock won't be complete without it.

Narrator: But why put yourself in danger for one sheep?

Shepherd: Because it knows I won't abandon it. It trusts me to bring it home.

Narrator: All right, what's its name then?

Shepherd: Basil.

Narrator: We'll help then.

All: (*With a 'Baa' in the voice*). Basil. Basil!

Shepherd: I think that I can hear him crying. Can you call his name again please?

All: Basil. Basil!

Shepherd: Here he is. He's down this deep hole. Don't worry Basil. I'll have you out in a jiffy.

All: Heave! Heave!

Shepherd: There you are everyone. I've got him safe. Come on Basil, time to go home.

Narrator: Hey, Shepherd. There's a woman here who's found a coin that she lost. Why don't you both have a party? After all, you've both found something precious that had gone missing. And that's why Jesus tells us that all the angels in heaven have a party when one person turns to God. Each of us is precious to him and he searches for us with all his might until he finds us and brings us home to be with him.

As with everything in worship, the primary purpose of drama is to please God, and there is a delicate balance between doing things as well as possible yet not minding when things go wrong. If drama is to be a regular feature, it is desirable, though not essential, to bring in someone with specialist knowledge. It is often difficult to find a leader who has both the necessary skills and the spiritual maturity. The answer to the first may lie in the many courses which are available; and one solution to the second is to link a less mature but creative leader with a church elder or staff team member who is weak on practical skills. Dance and drama can be administered 'under one umbrella' for it is often hard to see where one ends and the other begins.

The following are two examples of the way drama can be used briefly to reinforce teaching points. Both personalise ideas which come directly from the Bible, and this can be very powerful. They need careful preparation, but not much rehearsal. The first is a short sketch introducing a talk about love – a monologue which starts with someone flicking through a Bible.

Love. . . . Well. . . . Let's see . . . 1 Thessalonians 4:9,10 says I've got to love my brothers and sisters more. That lets me off the hook, I'm an only child. Or does it mean my brothers and sisters in Christ? Well, I *think* I can manage to love everyone who goes to *my* housegroup . . . and even all those who sit on *my* side of the church.

Now Leviticus 19:18 says I've got to love my neighbour. Well, I live at the end of my street so that only means the Green family and they're very nice. I can love my neighbour and actually I *think* I'm prepared to extend that to everyone on my street.

And Matthew 5:44 says I've got to love my enemies. But I'm not the sort to have any of those. Right, that seems to be it – church, neighbours, enemies.

Now (*flicking through Bible to check*) it doesn't seem to say I've got to love that awful Snoggs family round the corner. They aren't church – they aren't neighbours – they can't *really* be called enemies, and their front garden is an absolute disgrace. Thank heavens I don't have to love them. Oh, and that obnoxious man in the corner shop. I don't think he fits into any of these categories either. So I don't have to love him. Well, that's a relief, I must say. . . .

Another possibility is punctuate a talk with snatches of dialogue. For example, someone giving a talk on the life of David could be repeatedly interrupted by David himself. At each stage he is on the verge of an important event and is full of emotion. The speaker asks him several questions and each conversation ends with David dashing off somewhere. David is:

1 Puzzled when asked to leave the sheep and go home (1 Samuel 16:11).
2 Excited to be taking provisions to his brothers in the army (1 Samuel 17:17–18).
3 Afraid and running away from Saul (1 Samuel 19:8–17).
4 Sad because of Saul's death, yet anticipating being made king (2 Samuel 2:1,4).

The use of drama as a teaching tool is so effective because we receive information with our eyes as well as our ears, and retain even more when we have to speak, or act out, something ourselves. Because faith is about experience we must always be searching for more ways to 'get into our systems' what we do in worship. It could be said that drama is part of the very fabric of worship, an essential not an option. In some churches, a small act of communal drama takes place every week when, at the invitation of the leader, everyone shares a physical sign of greeting with those around them, using words such as 'The peace of God be with you'. There are many other imaginative ways of inviting people to participate dramatically in this way, although we should be aware that some find even 'passing the peace' threatening so, as ever, opting out is an equally valid option.

Testimonies and interviews

Nothing is more powerful than hearing someone's personal experience of God. Many of us have come to know Christ as a result of another's testimony, though if they are too long even the most inspiring of these can get slightly tedious! It is worth suggesting that people write their testimony down for, even if the notes are discarded, it can help inexperienced speakers decide exactly what they want to say. As far as possible they must be encouraged to use their own words and not to lapse into Christian cliches; those in leadership can encourage this by doing the same themselves! For obvious reasons it is tempting to put new Christians 'on show', but standing up in public makes them very vulnerable and this applies particularly to children. One suggestion which works well is an interview about some aspect of their faith which has already been talked about, perhaps in the privacy of a smaller group. It is helpful if children have the chance to go over any material with the interviewer beforehand, though not actually as a rehearsal. churches which are used to a lot of spontaneous sharing may occasionally need to build in some formality to ensure it is not always the same people who offer their personal experiences and that children's contributions are heard and valued.

Quizzes and games

Like Tabasco sauce, quizzes and games are to be used sparingly! Yet nothing is more effective for getting attention and stimulating thought than some sort of competition. Puzzles can be printed on the notice sheet to create a link between the service and the activity of home. Simple challenges such as, 'How many words can you make from the letters of HARVEST?' catch the imagination of all ages and the quick-witted speaker might integrate some of the answers into a talk. Quizzes can be used to teach Bible verses, by filling in missing letters (a 'hangman' type game), or gradually obliterating letters or words. The words of a text can be jumbled up and rearranged by a volunteer. True/False questions, in response to which people 'vote' by raising their hands, can introduce movement and underline teaching points. Or of course a quiz might be just for fun! It is important to check that a quiz is scheduled for a point in the service where we do want to stimulate people; perhaps as preparation for a talk or before children leave for peer group activities, rather than before a time of quiet singing or prayer. And it is not wise to push people too hard. A lady once said emphatically at the end of an all-age service, 'I do *not* want to play "Clumps" in the house of God, thank you very much.' And why should she?

DO be able to justify it – not just as a time filler.

DO explain the link with the rest of the worship.

DO be topical – adapt current TV games, etc.

DO make 'visuals' big enough for everyone to see.

DO allow it to be funny – earnest quiz leaders are bores.

DO score so there is real competition and a clear winner.

DO include questions where adults have no advantage over children.

DO use quizzes to check that people know *facts*.

DO target questions for special groups: eg, one for over 60s.

DO be critical of yourself.

DON'T expect it to achieve too much – it's OK to have a bit of fun.

DON'T go on too long and ruin a good idea with 'over-kill'.

DON'T use 'old favourites' which only the over-forties remember.

DON'T make anything too elaborate – it isn't worth the trouble.

DON'T forget you are leading worship.

DON'T 'fix' the scoring – it is devastating for children.

DON'T make it trivial – include the odd hard question.

DON'T make it feel like an exam – find novel ways of answering.

DON'T embarrass anyone – unless the minister enjoys being teased!

DON'T repeat it next week!

Decorating the church

Decorating the church building, particularly for festivals, is not to be compared with putting up the Christmas decorations at home or in the office. It is another chance to make use of symbolism; another opportunity for the generations to work together; another way of stimulating worship and thought. The Holy Spirit often reveals new sides to our personalities, bringing out creative gifts even in those who have bad memories of art at school. Everybody makes an effort at Christmas and Easter, but why not decorate the church at a time when people do not expect it? We are used to displays from children's groups, but why not invite house groups and other organisations to take their turn in flower arranging or making posters or banners. More and more churches are forming art groups to coordinate this and also subsidiary tasks, like notice boards and publicity.

Initiation ceremonies

In the Old Testament initiation was crucial, with circumcision ceremonies the excuse for much celebration, and baptism replaced this as the way both sexes entered the Christian church. It is good if we make much of events such as baptism, confirmation, dedication, thanksgiving and other ways by which churches admit people into the congregation or mark the birth of babies. All such occasions are so important that it is good for the whole church to be present. Children will then learn the custom of their particular church, start to put in context what might have happened to them in the past (dedication or infant baptism) and form some concept of what might happen in the future (adult baptism or confirmation and other ways of being admitted into adult membership). Many such services are long and wordy, so advice about how to make the most of the visual aspects of sacramental actions is given in the next chapter. The symbolic actions are, to say the least, as important as the credal statements and testimonies, and an all-age service will particularly focus on them.

Festivals and local celebrations

All humans have the need to celebrate in a festive, convivial way. Today many people do not live near their relatives, and at the main church festivals like Christmas and Easter, the make-up of a congregation may not be typical. There is a wealth of resource material available for use at such times, but it is sad that much Christmas worship is over before the season has really begun. One positive thing we can do is to make more of seasons such as Lent or Advent and the church's 'birthday' or founder's day or patronal festival. We can celebrate All Saints' Day as a more acceptable alternative to Hallowe'en. We can be aware of secular festivals like Father's Day and local events, not necessarily adding them to the Christian calendar but finding some appropriate way of using what is already in the minds of the participants. After all, the Christian church has always done this, and much of what we do at Christmas and at weddings originated in pagan customs!

The rhythm of the year is important, but we need not always celebrate the same occasions in the same way. Harvest is not only about rainbows or remembering the poor!

Festivals often attract non-regulars and it is important that we understand the role of 'folk religion' in our locality. The religion of any community is like an iceberg: regular worshippers show as the tip, but underneath lie a web of ideas, deeply felt but often unspoken. Countries have a formal 'national religion', expressed in occasions like royal weddings and state ceremonies and remembrance parades. Locally, folk religion centres on rituals concerning birth, marriage and death and is much concerned with family gatherings. It is resistant to change and often quite unreal, but it helps explain why there is such strength of feeling about the modernisation of church buildings or new forms of worship, even from people who never darken the church's door! Folk religion can be both an opening for God and a hindrance to the church's mission, but if we listen for it, it will teach us about the expectations of those who come to church just occasionally. Nowadays many people have almost no opportunity to experience worship of any sort, except on television and at funerals, and the under forties may not even know beyond the first line of the well-known carols! We must not blame them for reading what we consider wrong meanings into Christian symbols, for the church has often added to their confusion.

Ideally we will try to use folk religion as a 'bridge', letting grace affirm any faith we find, however incomplete. In Acts 10 we read of Peter taking the risk of offering the Gospel to the Gentile Cornelius even though it went against so much of what he had been taught. In Acts 17:27 we read that God decided where and when each person should live, 'so that they would look for him, and perhaps find him as they felt about for him.' Some with a very under-developed faith do occasionally 'feel about' for God by putting themselves within the influence of the church. The atmosphere of lively all-age worship may give the best opportunity for them to find the God they are looking for. After all, as William Temple said, the church is 'the only institution which exists for the sake of those who do not belong to it.'

9
COMMUNION

A letter from an eight-year-old child arrived recently at Scripture Union's London office. It read: 'I live in Keynsham and every Sunday I run into Sunday School and say hello, but sometimes I go to church when it is a family service. I sit with my mum and dad. Sometimes my mum gives me a polo out of her handbag and I pretend when we all go up to kneel at the front I eat it and pretend it is the body of Christ. When I have finished it I say my prays to God. From Alina.'

This letter provoked joy and sadness in equal measure! Had she been born in the first 1500 years of the existence of the Christian church, Alina would not have needed to resort to pretence. If her parents had been Henry VIII and Anne Boleyn, she would have been baptised, had hands laid on her as a mark of receiving the Holy Spirit, and then taken communion, at three days old. (Wine-soaked bread would have touched her lips – not even Elizabeth I had a suitable digestive system in infancy!) This is still the practice of Byzantine (Orthodox) churches, whose procedure in this matter provides an unbroken link to what was certainly the custom of the Christian churches in the fourth and fifth centuries, perhaps even beyond.

The history of children and communion

The change in practice came about not for theological reasons, but for administrative convenience! In the thirteenth century the significance of being filled with the Holy Spirit was in decline. The practice of laying hands on those who had been baptised, with prayers that they will receive the Holy Spirit, was being widely ignored. The bishops were anxious to restore the prominence of the Holy Spirit in the experience of believers. (This has a very contemporary ring about it!) At a meeting in Lambeth in 1281, it was decided that in order to give some tangible 'benefit' to this rite (called 'confirmation' in some churches), communion should only be received after the laying on of hands had taken place. Some time later there was a rearrangement of the church's administrative system which meant that bishops oversaw much larger areas. They could no longer be present at every baptism, so local church leaders (presbyters) were authorised to baptise, with bishops administering confirmation at massed events when the believers reached adulthood. Thus communion became an exclusively adult event almost by accident, and that pattern survived the Reformation and the rise of new denominations (including those which do not baptise infants) through five centuries.

The underlying assumption of all-age worship is that children are not just the church of tomorrow, they are the church of today; that children are a part of the body of Christ in just as real a sense as adult Christians. And the underlying assumption of this book is that they are church members not just in a passive or probationary sense, but in an active one. Prayer brings a church together, so we treat children as believers and pray alongside them; worship brings a church together so we treat children as believers and praise alongside them; but above all else communion brings a church together, so we . . . oh!

Some objections

'But children cannot *understand* communion!' protest those who wish to persist in excluding them. This suggests a misunderstanding of what communion is for. God chose to work the salvation of humankind in a way so complex that theologians have spent two millennia filling endless books which inch toward an understanding. Until Jesus returns, we will never fully comprehend what it was about his life, death and resurrection which won us reconciliation with God. Maybe we were never meant to. However, our gracious God has given us a way of apprehending what we can never comprehend; of accepting and experiencing what we cannot understand. Communion is so precious a memorial because practical 'doing' is infinitely easier than abstract 'thinking'; we take part in it precisely *because* we cannot understand! The illogic of this protest is seen even more clearly in churches where children are present for the part of a service during which communion is celebrated, but receive a blessing instead of bread and wine. Under these circumstances they are required to listen to a long and complicated prayer which precedes the administration (the cerebral part which they can't understand, but do not take part in the eating and drinking (the easy, experiential part which they could understand)!

We need to be aware, of course, of the seriousness of Paul's warning in 1 Corinthians 11:27–29, in which the Christians at Corinth are told that if they eat and drink 'without recognising the body of the Lord', they bring judgment upon themselves. What kind of 'unworthy' behaviour was Paul so concerned about that he called it 'sin against the body and blood of the Lord'? His accusations against the Corinthians were that they had despised the church, humiliated the poor, and treated the Lord's supper as an opportunity to over-eat and get drunk (verses 21–22). These are not the kinds of acts of naughtiness we recognise in children. It is we adults, with our vastly greater capacity for sin, who need to pay heed to Paul's warning. It seems hypocritical and patronising to rally to protect children from condemnation over this matter since their guilt for failing to share during worship must surely be related to their ability to sin in this way, an ability which clearly grows as believers mature and become more responsible. And of course, the shared dinner which the Corinthians would have experienced as their celebration of communion has developed into such a symbolic and individualised 'meal' that there is little sense of corporate giving and receiving in today's services.

What is the 'body of Christ' that we are instructed to recognise? Throughout the New Testament it is used as a metaphor for the church (Ephesians 4, for example). This body of Christ is not the church of tomorrow, but the church of today, the one we so often declare children to be part of alongside adults! We need to be quietly conscious of the fact that, if children do not receive communion, then it is not a celebration of the body of Christ – it is a celebration of three-quarters of the body of Christ. Is it possible that it is we adults who turn children away who have failed to 'recognise the body of the Lord'?

Possibilities for action

Change is inexorably underway. Moves to welcome children to communion are taking place across the world and across all denominations, including (to a lesser degree) those which do not baptise children. The speed at which progress is being made varies, and so does the detail. In some places, whole denominations are discussing how to introduce guidelines for admission of children in an orderly way (some of them settling on an arbitrary age at which inclusion is appropriate); in others, congregations are able unilaterally to decide what action is appropriate.

To begin with, some advice for those in churches where children do not participate in communion. First, encourage those who lead the church (the elders, the council, the pastorate, or whatever group is appropriate) to discuss the issue so that the church's policy is a definite one, not one which has come about through neglect. Second, ensure that proper teaching about the meaning of communion is given both to adults and children, especially if the church is one of the many where children never see it administered in the usual course of church life because they are elsewhere worshipping with their peer groups. Third, if children are present when communion takes place, make sure that they can at least see what happens. Jesus did not ask us to remember him with a prayer – he asked us to do something which can be seen, touched, tasted and smelt. Children (and indeed adults) should be encouraged to have their eyes open during the prayer which precedes administration so that they can see the bread being broken and so on. It may be appropriate to invite them to come forward and sit on the floor so that they can get a better view. Fourth, be aware that with the increasingly mobile population during this interim period between universal exclusion and universal inclusion, families will move from churches where children receive communion to churches where they do not. If such children come to your church and you intend to excommunicate them, have ready the pastoral help you will need in order to cope with the hurt and confusion that will be caused.

And some advice for those who intend to welcome children! If the rules of your denomination specify the age at which children may receive communion, respect them. Otherwise, decide and publicise the church's policy and practice so that this enriching activity does not accidentally become an embarrassing one. One common practice is for the administrator to give the bread and wine to a parent in the usual way, and then allow him or her to take the elements and distribute them to the rest of the family as seems appropriate. This is a most effective approach, both pastorally and practically. It does not, however, solve the problem of the child who is sent to church by non-attending parents – perhaps even against his or her will. Experience has shown, though, that when time is spent individually with such a child, explaining why the congregation is taking part in this unique activity and cautiously bearing in mind the expectations of non-attending parents, he or she is able to decide quite sincerely whether or not it is right to be a part of it. One-to-one explanations like this are time-consuming, but they are valuable. Even a simple decision that a child does not want to feel excluded when the people of God are all doing something special is a mark of God's grace and a small act of faith – and in these circumstances the children's group leader who had the conversation can stand in for the parent at the administration.

The comments about ensuring that children can see apply equally here. When, before the Reformation, the preparation of the bread and the wine took place far from the congregation, only to be glimpsed tantalisingly and heard in mumbled Latin, a vast and unhelpful mysteriousness grew around the ritual. 'Hoc est corpus', the priest would whisper, leaving the congregation wondering what magic the 'hocus-pocus' they were hearing about did to the bread. We want children and adults to see what is going on and to understand why it is happening. The focus must be on the actions, not the words. So, although we need serious and explanatory prayers before the administration, they need to be short when children are present so that inability to concentrate does not prevent God and the congregation communicating with each other. The last thing we want is for people to conclude that the spoken explanation and prayer are more significant than the action! In this respect, it is encouraging to see those denominations which follow a written liturgy struggling to provide suitably accessible words and structures. It is wise to make full use of the simpler and shorter patterns for worship as they become available.

And finally, you may need to ensure that the elements

themselves are of a suitable nature for those who will consume them. Many churches use a non-alcoholic wine, or give children just the bread (historically it has always been acceptable even for adults only to receive one element).

We need to bear in mind, of course, that welcoming children to communion does not solve all problems. It may even exaggerate the difficulty that teenagers feel in finding their own place in the life of a church. At some point they need to ask themselves whether they want to confirm as their own the practices they have accepted as habit, their origins perhaps buried so far in their pasts that they cannot remember when or why they began. Their confusion may become greater when they realise that other churches do not give communion to people of their age. As in every area of the life of a multi-generational church, we need to allow teenagers the space to make their own decisions in their own ways – even if those ways seem awkward or unhelpful. And that space includes the continued availability of non-judgmental pastoral advice – and the right to decline the advice if it is not wanted!

The never-ending story

Churches are organised by adults. That is how it should be! But they must not be organised for adults; they must be organised for all! As soon as children are born they need to be treated as they are – at one with adults in the love of Christ, at one with adults in the body of Christ. We want them to be aware that, with their family or, later on, their peer group, they have never been anything less than fully accepted as part of the local worshipping community. A vision is forming for children growing up with no concept of a first visit to church nor even a first communion. That event would have taken place deep in infancy, and become a basic rhythm of life, the beginning of which is far beyond the child's ability to recall. Indeed, we long to see households where children are so used to going through life with Christ as Lord, that it is only when mixing for the first time with peers outside the church, for example at a pre-school playgroup, that they discover inadvertently that there are others who try to get by without Jesus!

However, this church would not be an exclusive one. It would be one where strangers find an immediate and engaging welcome. If they live as individuals they would be met with a non-threatening invitation to find support and company in groups. If they live as families they would be encouraged to discover God's love together, their first experience of church not being segregation on the basis of their ages, but a welcome to enjoy encountering God in the security of each others' company.

Nor would it be a church where the needs of children dominate its life so much that the elderly find the personal attention to their needs which gave them value is snatched away. Instead their accumulated wisdom would be tapped and their preference for developments to take place at a dignified pace recognised.

This is the church for all ages. The church whose worship and learning is simple, not embarrassingly childish, but visual and interactive. The church for people who arrive as outsiders, but find their needs so appropriately met that they wonder how they managed without. The church for people whose presence is so continuously appreciated into old age that it is secure on a foundation of rich experience. This church for all ages is not a dream to be wistful for, it is a vision to pursue.

Paul wrote to one of the churches he had visited because he wanted every man, woman and child of them to be 'built together to become a dwelling in which God lives by his Spirit' (Ephesians 2:22). That is why we have written, too!

Part Two
RESOURCES

The resources in this section are categorised into the different ways a congregation may want to approach God during an all-age service. Some are designed for use in structured or liturgical settings; some invite spontaneous participation and are more suitable for unstructured worship. They have in common the use of the Bible as their source or their inspiration. Not every word of every one will be understood by young children (this is all-age worship, not children's worship). However, they are simple, often repetitive and invite people of all ages to find in them different levels of meaning.

Contents

1
PRAISE

For the earth's beauty

Everyone responds to the leader with the words in *italics:*

God has filled the earth with beauty.
All the world, give God your praises.
Worship is your joy and duty.
All the world, give God your praises.
Who filled up the sea with water?
All the world, give God your praises.
Made each child a son or daughter?
All the world, give God your praises.
Made cows moo and set snakes hissing?
All the world, give God your praises.
Who invented hugs and kissing?
All the world, give God your praises.
Who decided stars would twinkle?
All the world, give God your praises.
Eyes would wink and foreheads wrinkle?
All the world, give God your praises.
Whose idea were films and telly?
All the world, give God your praises.
Who makes Stilton cheese so smelly?
All the world, give God your praises.
Only God could be that clever,
All the world, give God your praises.
Let his praises sound forever.
All the world, give God your praises.

God's greatness

The leader should repeatedly say: 'Lord your greatness fills . . .', inserting the names of all the surrounding towns and villages. After each, the congregation responds with the words of Psalm 8:9: 'O Lord, our Lord, your greatness is seen in all the world.'

Noisy praise

In the manner of Psalm 148:7–10, call on all creation to praise God. Follow this pattern, adding four or five animals:

Leader: The sheep praise you by saying:
Young children: Baa!
All: Let them all praise the name of the Lord.
Leader: The cows praise you by saying:
Young children: Moo!
All: Let them all praise the name of the Lord.

Song of creation

For several voices.

A: Bless the Lord, created things; angels in heaven;
All: Sing God's praise and exalt him forever.
B: Clouds in the sky; sun, moon and stars.
All: Sing God's praise and exalt him forever.
C: Bless the Lord, light and darkness; rain, dew and wind;
All: Sing God's praise and exalt him forever.
A: Frost, ice and snow; lightning and storms.
All: Sing God's praise and exalt him forever.
B: Bless the Lord, hills and flat land; rivers and seas;
All: Sing God's praise and exalt him forever.
C: Plants, animals, fish, birds, people.
All: Sing God's praise and exalt him forever.

Using Jeremiah 31:35

Read the verse together as a shout of praise to God: 'The Lord provides sun for light by day, the moon and stars to shine by night. He stirs up the sea and makes it roar; his name is the Lord Almighty.'

Using Luke 1:68–79

The congregation responds to the leader with the italic lines:

The family of David
Has produced a mighty Saviour,
The prophets told us that he'd
Come to deal with bad behaviour,
Now praise the God of Israel, who sets his people free.
God promised long ago that
He'd show mercy in these days,
And set us free to worship,
Without fear to give him praise,
Now praise the God of Israel, who sets his people free.
A prophet has been born
And he has come the way to pave
For God to bring forgiveness
To the ones he longs to save,
Now praise the God of Israel, who sets his people free.
In tenderness and mercy
God brings everyone release,
From shadows gently guides
Our steps into the way of peace,
Now praise the God of Israel, who sets his people free.
All glory to the Father
And the Spirit and the Son,
And this is how it shall be
'Til our time on earth is done,
Now praise the God of Israel, who sets his people free.

Praising Jesus

Invite the congregation to cluster into groups of two or three by turning on their seats, so that they can talk to the people alongside whom they are sitting, children and adults together. Ask them to remember as many things as possible that Jesus did which suggest that he was the Son of God, e.g. he walked on water, healed the sick, rose from the dead. After about a minute ask people to call out the things they have thought of, while someone makes a list on an overhead projector or chart. This list may be used in several ways:

1 In an open time of praise, invite children or adults to choose one fact from the list and say: 'Praise you, Jesus, that you . . .'

2 The leader says a prayer which includes the suggestions of the congregation.

3 In a responsive act of praise, the leader repeatedly says: 'Thank you, Jesus, that you. . .'. Each time the congregation replies: 'You are the Christ, the Son of God.'

4 The same pattern could be followed, asking groups to think of names by which Jesus is known, e.g, Prince of Peace, Emmanuel, Lamb of God.

5 Alternatively, think of adjectives that describe Jesus, e.g., holy, loving, glorious, compassionate.

The living Jesus

Night comes at the end of the day,
But Jesus is alive,
Spring and summer pass away,
But Jesus is alive,
Suns burn out and black the sky,
But Jesus is alive,
Knights and heroes fade and die,
But Jesus is alive,
Songs are gone as soon as sung,
But Jesus is alive,
Many people die too young,
But Jesus is alive,
Stars lose fame as fast as youth,
But Jesus is alive,
Cling to this eternal truth,
That Jesus is alive.

Using Psalm 72:18–19

Leader: Praise the Lord, the God of Israel!
All: He alone does wonderful things.
Leader: Praise his glorious name forever!
All: May his glory fill the world.
Leader: Amen! Amen!
All: Amen! Amen!

Praising the Trinity

Women: Praise to God, our heavenly Father,
Men: Praise to Christ, his only Son,
Young people: Praise to God, the Holy Spirit,
All: Always three and ever one.
Women: Praise and worship to the Father,
Men: Praise and worship to the Son,
Young people: Praise and worship to the Spirit,
All: Holy God, the living one. Alleluia!

For Christ's glory

As the sun in all its brightness,
Such is Jesus Christ in glory,
As the snow in all its whiteness,
Such is Jesus Christ in glory,
As the lightning, as the thunder,
Such is Jesus Christ in glory,
As the sky at night in wonder,
Such is Jesus Christ in glory,
As the ocean in its deepness,
Such is Jesus Christ in glory,
As the mountain in its steepness,
Such is Jesus Christ in glory,
As the hurricane in power,
Such is Jesus Christ in glory,
As the beauty of the flower,
Such is Jesus Christ in glory,
As the rich, lifegiving blood,
Such is Jesus Christ in glory,
Utterly, supremely God,
Such is Jesus Christ in glory.

God's powerful presence

Establish a rhythm for this praise chant by clapping hands, clicking fingers or stamping feet. Repeat these words many times, starting fairly quietly, then building up the volume until the word 'now' is shouted:

God is great,
God is powerful,
God is with us NOW.

Based on Isaiah 12

Leader: A day is coming when people will say,
All: I praise you, Lord.
Leader: You were angry with us,
All: But now you comfort us and are angry no longer.
Leader: God is our Saviour.
All: We will trust him and not be afraid.
Leader: The Lord gives us power and strength.
All: He is our Saviour.
Leader: Just as fresh water brings joy to the thirsty.
All: So God's people rejoice when he saves us.
Leader: Give thanks to the Lord!
All: We call on him to help us!
Leader: Tell all the nations what he has done.
All: We will tell them how great he is.
Leader: Sing to the Lord because of the great things he has done.
All: Let the whole world hear the news.
Leader: Let everyone alive shout and sing,
All: God lives among his people!

Based on Nehemiah 9:5–6

Leader: Stand up and praise the Lord your God;
All: Praise him forever and ever!
Leader: Let everyone praise his glorious name;
All: No human praise is great enough.
Leader: You made the heavens and the stars of the sky;
All: You made land and sea and everything in them.
Leader: You give life to all; the heavenly powers bow down and worship you;
All: You Lord, you alone are God.

Simple song for young children

To the tune of 'Frère Jacques':

God the true God, God the true God,
He is Lord, he is Lord,
Father, Son and Spirit, Father, Son and Spirit,
Thank you God, thank you God.

Another song for young children

To the tune of 'Ring a ring o' roses':

We can sing for Jesus,
We can sing for Jesus,
Hosanna! Hosanna!
We all praise the King.

Jesus the Saviour

Jesus born in poverty, Jesus friend to the needy, Jesus healer
of the sick. Alleluia!
Our Saviour and our King.
Jesus riding in triumph, Jesus hailed as leader, Jesus
welcomed as Messiah. Alleluia!
Our Saviour and our King.
Jesus deserted by his friends, Jesus treated as a criminal,
Jesus lied about and insulted. Alleluia!
Our Saviour and our King.
Jesus suffering on the cross, Jesus dying in our place, Jesus
raised to life victoriously. Alleluia!
Our Saviour and our King.
Jesus present with us now, Jesus hope for our world, Jesus
Lord for all eternity. Alleluia!
Our Saviour and our King.

With the Spirit's help

Holy Spirit help us pray,
Give to God the praise and glory,
Fill us all with power today,
Give to God the praise and glory,
Though we cannot see, we know,
Give to God the praise and glory,
You are here like years ago,
Give to God the praise and glory,
Give us voices full of praise,
Give to God the praise and glory,
Pleasing God in many ways,
Give to God the praise and glory.

For the ascended Jesus

Leader: Ascended Lord Jesus,
All: We praise you and adore you.
Leader: Once you lived a brief life on earth,
All: Now you are the same yesterday, today and forever.
Leader: Once you lived in a small Middle Eastern country,
All: Now you are with all Christians in every place.
Leader: Once you showed your love to those you met.
All: Now your love is poured out through all the universe.
Leader: Ascended Lord Jesus, through the power of your Spirit,
All: We praise you and adore you.

Perfect man and holy God

Leader: Lord Jesus Christ, we worship you, the Son of God.
All: There is no other god but you.
Leader: Lord Jesus Christ, we worship you, the Son of Man.
All: There is no other man like you.
Leader: No matter how wise anyone is,
All: You are wiser, for you know everything.
Leader: No matter how strong anyone is,
All: You are stronger, for you are our powerful God.
Leader: Perfect man and holy God,
All: We worship you. Amen.

Using Psalm 105

Leader: Give thanks to the Lord.
All: We will proclaim his greatness.
Leader: Tell the nations what he has done.
All: We will sing praise to the Lord.
Leader: Tell of the wonderful things he has done.
All: We are glad that we belong to God.
Leader: Let all who worship him rejoice.
All: We will go to the Lord for help.
Leader: Worship him continually.
All: We declare publicly that the Lord is our God.

Using Psalm 24:1

The world and all that is in it belongs to the Lord,
The world and all that is in it belongs to the Lord,
The dads, the mums and the children belong to the Lord,
The world and all that is in it belongs to the Lord,
The cats, the dogs and the gerbils belong to the Lord,
The world and all that is in it belongs to the Lord,
The sisters, the brothers and cousins belong to the Lord,
The world and all that is in it belongs to the Lord,
The grans, grandpas and lodgers belong to the Lord,
The world and all that is in it belongs to the Lord,
The friends, the colleagues and neighbours belong to the
  Lord,
The world and all that is in it belongs to the Lord,

Based on Jonah 2

Leader: In our distress, Lord, we call to you,
All: And you answer us.
Leader: We cry for help,
All: And you hear us.
Leader: O Lord, we pray to you,
All: And in your holy temple you listen to us.
Leader: We will sing praises to you,
All: We will offer you a sacrifice of praise.
Leader: We will do what we have promised,
All: Salvation comes from the Lord.

King of kings

Leader: Powerful Jesus,
All: Your strength is greater than ours.
Leader: Wise Jesus,
All: Your thoughts are more wonderful than ours.
Leader: Caring Jesus,
All: Your love is deeper than ours.
Leader: We make you our Lord,
All: Because there is no one else like you.
Leader: There are many kings,
All: But you are King of the kings.
Leader: There are hundreds of lords,
All: But you are Lord of the lords.

Based on Psalm 148

You that live in heaven above,
Praise the Lord, praise the Lord,
All his angels and heavenly armies,
Praise the Lord, praise the Lord,
Sun, moon and shining stars,
Praise the Lord, praise the Lord,
Highest heaven and waters that fall from the sky,
Praise the Lord, praise the Lord,
Sea creatures and all ocean depths,
Praise the Lord, praise the Lord,
Lightning and hail, snow and clouds,
Praise the Lord, praise the Lord,
Strong winds that obey his commands,
Praise the Lord, praise the Lord,
Let them praise the name of the Lord, for he commanded
  and they were created,
Praise the Lord, praise the Lord.

Based on 2 Chronicles 5:13

Establish a rhythm by clicking fingers, then say the words:
'Praise the Lord for he is good, his love goes on for ever
more.' The finger-click comes on the off-beat ('the', 'for',
'is', 'his', etc.). Repeat it four times, louder each time.

Hosanna!

Proclaim with me the Lord's greatness, let us praise his
  name together . . .
Praise God! Hosanna!
Praise him, all you who obey him . . .
Praise God! Hosanna!
The Lord, the most high, for he is a great king . . .
Praise God! Hosanna!
He is clothed with majesty and strength . . .
Praise God! Hosanna!
He rules over the whole earth . . .
Praise God! Hosanna!
For those who honour the Lord, his love lasts forever . . .
Praise God! Hosanna!
God bless those who come in the name of the Lord . . .
Praise God! Hosanna!

Based on Deuteronomy 32:3–4

I will praise the name of the Lord.
Praise the God of all justice.
His people will tell of his greatness.
Praise the God of all justice.
The Lord is your mighty defender.
Praise the God of all justice.
Perfect and just are all his ways.
Praise the God of all justice.
Your God is faithful and true.
Praise the God of all justice.
He does what is right and fair.
Praise the God of all justice.

Awareness of God

Lord God, you are in my world,
You fill it through and through,
Your presence offers peace,
Lord God, you are in my nation,
You fill it through and through,
Your presence offers peace,
Lord God, you are in my church,
You fill it through and through,
Your presence offers peace,
Lord God, you are in my home,
You fill it through and through,
Your presence offers peace,
Lord God, you are in my life,
You fill it through and through,
Your presence offers peace.

Praise that goes with a bang

Distribute six balloons to members of the congregation and invite them to stand at the front. The balloons bear letters which together make up the word PRAISE, and inside each is a piece of paper bearing the words of a Bible verse about praising God, placed there before the balloon was inflated. One at a time, invite the six to burst their balloons and read out the verse: suggested verses are Psalm 92:1, Psalm 95:1, Psalm 96:2, 2 Corinthians 1:3, Philippians 1:11, 1 Peter 1:3.

Based on Psalm 104

Leader: Praise the Lord, my soul!
All: O Lord my God, how great you are!
Leader: You have made so many things.
All: How wisely you made them all.
Leader: The earth is filled with your creatures.
All: All of them depend on you.
Leader: You provide food and we are satisfied.
All: You give new life to the earth.
Leader: May the glory of the Lord last forever!
All: May the Lord be happy with what he has made!
Leader: As long as I live I will sing praises to God.
All: May he be pleased with my song.
Leader: Praise the Lord, my soul!
All: All my gladness comes from him.

Using Psalm 18:1–3

Split the congregation into two groups:

A: How I love you Lord!
B: You are my defender.
A: The Lord is my protector;
B: He is my strong fortress.
A: My God is my protection,
B: And I am safe with him.
A: He protects me like a shield;
B: He defends me and keeps me safe.
A: I call to the Lord,
B: And he saves me from my enemies.
All: Praise the Lord!

Putting Jesus in his rightful place

Jesus Lord of all, you are so powerful, and we are so weak
. . .
Holy Jesus, we worship you.
You are so important, and we are so unimportant . . .
Holy Jesus, we worship you.
You are so perfect, and we are so sinful . . .
Holy Jesus, we worship you.
You are so loving, and we are so selfish . . .
Holy Jesus, we worship you.
You are so wise, and we are so foolish . . .
Holy Jesus, we worship you.
You are our leader, and we will gladly follow . . .
Holy Jesus, we worship you.

Emmanuel: God is with us

Eternal God, but born as a human baby. God has stepped
into our world.
Jesus, we praise and adore you.
Light of all the universe, but born in the darkness of a stable.
God has stepped into our world.
Jesus, we praise and adore you.
Born in a Jewish family, but Saviour for every nation. God
has stepped into our world.
Jesus, we praise and adore you.
Bringer of hope and fulfilment, but rejected by so many.
God has stepped into our world.
Jesus, we praise and adore you.
Crucified, but risen again in glory. God has stepped into
our world.
Jesus, we praise and adore you.

The plan of God

God is working out his plan,
God is powerful, praise him, praise him,
Started before time began,
God is powerful, praise him, praise him,
Formed a nation for his own,
God is powerful, praise him, praise him,
Made to worship him alone,
God is powerful, praise him, praise him,
Sent his Son to set us free,
God is powerful, praise him, praise him,
Rose from death, triumphantly
God is powerful, praise him, praise him,
Still as strong as that today,
God is powerful, praise him, praise him,
Loud as we can shout, let's say,
God is powerful, praise him, praise him.

Based on Psalm 147:1–11

Leader: It is good to sing praise to our God,
All: It is pleasant and right to praise him.
Leader: He heals the broken-hearted,
All: And bandages their wounds.
Leader: He knows the number of stars,
All: He has a name for each one of them.
Leader: Great and mighty is our Lord,
All: His wisdom cannot be measured.
Leader: Sing hymns of praise to the Lord,
All: Play the guitars for our God.
Leader: He takes pleasure in those who put him first,
All: We trust in his constant love.

2
THANKSGIVING

For our senses

The congregation responds to the leader with the words in italics:

When I see the Concorde flying,
Life is lovely thanks to God,
Sunset as the day is dying,
Life is lovely thanks to God,
Hear the roar of crowds at Wembley,
Life is lovely thanks to God,
Roller-coasters turn me trembly,
Life is lovely thanks to God,
Trumpets sounding brash and tinny,
Life is lovely thanks to God,
Hot baths round me bare and skinny,
Life is lovely thanks to God,
Dewdrops hung on cobweb wisps,
Life is lovely thanks to God,
Taste of ready-salted crisps,
Life is lovely thanks to God,
Smell of eggs and bacon cooking,
Life is lovely thanks to God,
Scratch an itch when no one's looking,
Life is lovely thanks to God,
Staying up till late at night,
Life is lovely thanks to God,
Then I shout with all my might,
Life is lovely thanks to God.

For the best things in creation

Invite the congregation to cluster into groups. Ask them to discuss: 'What is, to you, the most wonderful thing in creation?' After a couple of minutes, ask a few to call out suggestions, then begin a time of thanks, either with spontaneous contributions from the congregation or by mentioning each item, followed by the response:

Leader: God, you have made all things well.
All: You are the Lord and we thank you.

For breakfast

Ask: 'What did you have for breakfast?' Thank God for the farmers who grow it, the workers in the factory, the truck drivers who deliver it, the people in the supermarket, and so on.

For God's knowledge of us

Based on Psalm 139:

Lord, you know everything I do. You see me when I work
and when I rest. Thank you, Lord God . . .
You know all about me.
You know what I am thinking and what I am going to say.
Thank you, Lord God . . .
You know all about me.
Even before I was born and even when I am grown up.
Thank you, Lord God . . .
You know all about me.
You are all around me and you protect me. Thank you,
Lord God . . .
You know all about me.
Wherever I go you will be there to help me. Thank you,
Lord God . . .
You know all about me.
From before I was born to the end of my days. Thank you,
Lord God . . .
You know all about me.
For knowing me and caring for me, thank you, Lord
God . . .
You know all about me.

For God's love

Especially suitable for young children:

Leader: Give me an L!
All: L!
Leader: Give me an O!
All: O!
Leader: Give me a V!
All: V!
Leader: Give me an E!
All: E!
Leader: Give me an S!
All: S!
Leader: What does God the Father do?
All: He loves me!
Leader: Give me a T!
All: T!
Leader: Give me an H!
All: H!
Leader: Give me an A!
All: A!
Leader: Give me an N!
All: N!
Leader: Give me a K!
All: K!
Leader: What do I do for God the Father?
All: I thank him!

For God's promises

Invite members of the congregation to call out things that God has promised us (e.g., never to leave us, to love us, to return to earth). Display the words: 'Thank you, God, that you have promised . . .' Invite anyone in the congregation to say prayers of thanksgiving which complete that phrase in a few words. The leader should close by reading Psalm 119:162.

For God's provision

The congregation repeats this prayer, line by line, after the leader:

Thank you, Lord God, that you love us;
Thank you, Lord God, for sending Jesus into our world;
Thank you, Lord God, that you want to rescue us from all that is wrong;
Thank you, Lord God, that no-one is too bad for you to help them;
Thank you, Lord God, that you know who I am and what I need;
Thank you, Lord God, because we are lost without you.

For people of all ages

When I've only just been born,
While I feed or cry or yawn,
Fill me, Lord, with thanks to you,
When I've grown a little older,
And my toddling's getting bolder,
Fill me, Lord, with thanks to you,
In my school days as a child,
Through my learning, tears and smiles,
Fill me, Lord, with thanks to you,
In my teenages and youth,
Fall in love and search for truth,
Fill me, Lord, with thanks to you,
Growing through my middle life,
Parent, single, husband, wife,
Fill me, Lord, with thanks to you,
Then, as older years draw on,
Experience to call upon,
Fill me, Lord, with thanks to you,
Faithful through my autumn days,
Looking back and full of praise,
Fill me, Lord, with thanks to you,
When my closing years are nearing,
Frail perhaps but persevering,
Fill me, Lord, with thanks to you.

For Jesus' unforgettable acts

Jesus our Saviour, out of your great love for us, you came to live on our planet. Thank you, Lord Jesus. . . .
We'll never forget it.

The night before you died, you gave us a meal so that we could remember you. Thank you, Lord Jesus . . .
We'll never forget it.

Then cruel men took you, beat you and told lies about you. Thank you, Lord Jesus . . .
We'll never forget it.

You died on a cross, even though it was we who deserved it. Thank you, Lord Jesus . . .
We'll never forget it.

But you rose to life again and defeated death once and for all. Thank you, Lord Jesus . . .
We'll never forget it.

As your forgiven people, we will live with you forever. Thank you, Lord Jesus . . .
We'll never forget it.

For our gifts

On a large piece of paper or overhead projector, 'brainstorm' skills and gifts that particular members of the congregation have – a spread of job skills, domestic skills and personal qualities. Invite people to keep their eyes open, looking at the list as the leader prays, thanking God that he makes us all so different, remembering that we all need each other, and praying for those who have not yet decided what they will do in life. Alternatively, make the gifts God has given to us the subject of a time of open thanksgiving.

For food

Ask the congregation to form small groups. Invite them to tell each other what they are going to have for lunch or, if they do not know yet, what they would most like to eat. After a minute, introduce a time of prayer during which anyone may say, loud enough for all to hear, 'Thank you, Lord, for . . . (*a favourite food*)'. Encourage the congregation to do so before every meal as a habit.

For water

Ask the congregation to call out things that water is used for in daily life. Write a list of these. In a time of prayer the leader should name the functions of water (eg, water is needed to make us clean), following each statement with:

Leader: For your gift of water,
All: We thank you, Lord God.

For each other

Give the congregation a chance to think in silence whether there is anything for which they want to say a personal thank you to another member of the fellowship or someone with whom they came to church that day. It might be something for which a loving thank you is long overdue, or simply a message of appreciation. Then encourage them to get up, find the person and deliver their thanks. If they need a specific phrase, suggest the words of Philippians 1:3: 'I thank my God for you'. Make it plain that some will prefer to stay seated and express their thanks privately to God.

For all kinds of weather

Ask the congregation to form groups, children and adults together, to make a list of all the types of weather they can think of. After some time, ask them to call out their answers and make a joint list. The leader should thank God for each one, stressing how valuable a part of God's creation it is, for example, 'Thank you, God, for lightning, because electricity is so useful to us.'

For your congregation

Ask everyone to find out the names of the people next to them and be ready to shout them at the right moment. The leader should read Philippians 1:3: 'I thank my God for you every time I think of you'. She should then pause while all the names are spoken simultaneously. When the hubbub has died away, she reads Philippians 1:4–5: 'Every time I pray for you all, I pray with joy because of the way in which you have helped me in the work of the gospel from the very first day until now.'

3
CONFESSION

Deeds, words and thoughts

The congregation responds to the reader with the repeated italic line:

This is a true saying, to be completely accepted and believed: 'Jesus Christ came into the world to save sinners'. So let us turn to God and find forgiveness, for we have sinned against him and do not deserve to be called his children.
Merciful Father, we confess to you the wrong things we have done.
Forgive us, Lord, for we are sorry.
We confess to you the wrong things we have said.
Forgive us, Lord, for we are sorry.
We confess to you the wrong things we have thought.
Forgive us, Lord, for we are sorry.
And we confess to you the things we have failed to do, failed to say, and failed to think.
Forgive us, Lord, for we are sorry. Amen.

Remembering God's justice

Explain that the confession will be divided into three parts. Ask the congregation to bring to mind something that is unfair in their family or school life. After a few seconds of silence, invite them to echo this prayer, phrase by phrase: 'God of justice, this angers you . . . ; God of justice, forgive us . . . ; God of justice, put right what is wrong. . .'. Then ask them to think of something unfair in the nation, repeating the silence and the phrases. Thirdly, ask them to reflect on an injustice in the way the world has developed, and continue as before.

Based on Daniel 9:4–19

Leader: Let us pray to the Lord our God and confess our sins.

All: Lord God, you are great and we honour you.

Leader: You are faithful and show constant love to those who love you.

All: We have done wrong.

Leader: We have rejected what you commanded us to do.

All: We have turned away from what you showed us was right.

Leader: We did not listen to you, O Lord our God.

All: But you are merciful and forgiving.

Leader: Lord, hear us.

All: Lord, forgive us.

Leader: In order that everyone will know that you are God,

All: Lord, forgive us and do not delay. Amen.

Our failures

For times when we have deliberately done things which we know you have forbidden,

Lord God, we are so sorry.

For times when we knew the right thing to do, but decided not to do it,

Lord God, we are so sorry.

For times when the situation was so difficult that we could barely help doing wrong,

Lord God, we are so sorry.

For times when our words and actions have hurt those who love us,

Lord God, we are so sorry.

For times when we simply haven't put much effort into following you,

Lord God, we are so sorry.

When we act like Jesus' enemies

Leader: Alone of all humankind, Jesus never did anything
wrong. But some people hated him enough to plot his
death. For the times we hate, or lie, or think badly, Lord,
forgive us.

All: Forgive us and help us.

Leader: Some people were pleased when Jesus died because
it would make life more convenient. For the times when
we are glad that bad things happen to others, Lord, forgive
us.

All: Forgive us and help us.

Leader: Some people were too scared or too careless to step
in and save Jesus. For times when we fail to speak out
for others who are treated badly, Lord, forgive us.

All: Forgive us and help us.

Leader: Some people hardly noticed what was going on
when Jesus was crucified. For times when we are too
busy to bother with God, Lord, forgive us.

All: Forgive us and help us. Amen.

When we let Jesus down

Lord Jesus, we confess to you that we have let you down.
When we stayed silent, but knew we should say
something, we have denied and failed you.

We are sorry, Lord; forgive us.

When we spoke, but knew that what we said was cowardly
or hurt someone, we have denied and failed you.

We are sorry, Lord; forgive us.

When we acted as though you meant nothing to us, we
have denied and failed you.

We are sorry, Lord; forgive us.

When we kept you trapped on Sunday, and didn't let you
affect the rest of our week, we have denied and failed
you.

We are sorry, Lord; forgive us.

When we had a chance to tell someone about you, but lost
our nerve, we have denied and failed you.

We are sorry, Lord; forgive us.

Lord Jesus, we know we have done wrong. As forgiven
people, help us to serve you better. Amen.

O Jesus, I have promised . . .

'O Jesus, I have promised to serve you to the end.' But sometimes we don't live up to the things we eagerly tell God we are prepared to do for him. Help us serve you better, Lord.

Forgive us all, we pray.

'Be now and ever near me, my Master and my friend.' But even though you stay near us, we behave as if you are not our friend. Help us serve you better, Lord.

Forgive us all, we pray.

'I shall not fear the battle, if you are by my side.' But often when it is hard to be a Christian we give up and do what is easiest instead. Help us serve you better, Lord.

Forgive us all, we pray.

'Nor wander from the pathway if you will be my guide.' But when temptation gets tough, we sometimes follow a path which we know is wrong and do things we know will make you sad. Help us serve you better, Lord.

Forgive us all, we pray.

Based on Psalm 51

Leader: Be merciful to us, O God, because of your constant love.

All: Because of your great mercy, wipe away our sins.

Leader: Wash away all our evil.

All: Make us clean from our sin.

Leader: We recognise our faults.

All: We are always conscious of our sins.

Leader: Remove our sins and we will be clean.

All: Wash us and we will be whiter than snow.

Leader: Create pure hearts in us, O God.

All: Put a new and loyal spirit in us.

Leader: Give us the joy that comes from your salvation,

All: And make us willing to obey you,

Leader: Then we will teach people your commands,

All: And we will turn back to you.

Leader: We will gladly proclaim your righteousness,

All: And we will praise you.

For waste and selfishness

God our Father, we are sorry that we have used your gifts
carelessly. When we enjoy eating and drinking, but forget
that you provide it all, Father in your mercy,
Forgive us and help us.
When we are full up, but forget the fact that millions are
hungry, Father in your mercy,
Forgive us and help us.
When we waste food because it isn't exactly what we want,
Father in your mercy,
Forgive us and help us.
When we have parties for those who will invite us back,
forgetting those who can't manage to repay us, Father in
your mercy,
Forgive us and help us.
When we give things because we hope people will think
highly of us, Father in your mercy,
Forgive us and help us.
So long as one person in our congregation is lonely, one
person in our area is needy, one person on our planet is
starving, Father in your mercy,
Forgive us and help us.

In certainty of forgiveness

Because Jesus has risen to life, sin has lost its power to keep
us away from God. So let us tell God we are sorry for
our sins, in certainty that he will forgive us and welcome
us as his friends. Because Jesus has risen . . .
Forgive us, Lord, we pray.
Let us confess the wrong things we have done. Because
Jesus has risen . . .
Forgive us, Lord, we pray.
Let us confess the wrong things we have said. Because Jesus
has risen . . .
Forgive us, Lord, we pray.
Let us confess the wrong things we have thought. Because
Jesus has risen . . .
Forgive us, Lord, we pray. Amen.

For the way we abuse God's creation

We are sorry we have spoiled your world.
Forgive us, Father, and help us.

Let us say sorry for the way people have spoiled what God created. For the pollution we cause by throwing rubbish on the land, sewage and chemicals into our waters, and harmful gasses into the atmosphere. We are sorry we have spoiled your world.
Forgive us, Father, and help us.

For the changes in climate that have come about because of our lifestyle; the holes in the ozone layer, the growth of deserts, the flooding due to forests being cut down. We are sorry we have spoiled your world.
Forgive us, Father, and help us.

For the greed which makes some countries take more than their fair share of food and resources. We are sorry we have spoiled your world.
Forgive us, Father, and help us.

For the irresponsibility and political intrigue which often prevents anything being done. We are sorry we have spoiled your world.
Forgive us, Father, and help us.

For the fact that it is always the poor who suffer most. We are sorry we have spoiled your world.
Forgive us, Father, and help us.

Turning in repentance

The leader says this prayer:

'Lord God, you promise to forgive all who are sorry for their sins. From the wrong things we have done, we turn away; please forgive us. From the wrong things we have said, we turn away; please forgive us. From the wrong things we have thought, we turn away; please forgive us. Amen!

He or she should then walk to the back of the room and invite the congregation to stand and turn around as a symbol of their decision to turn away from sin to Jesus, who forgives them. Psalm 32:1–2 and 11 are read.

Knowing we are forgiven

We've all done wrong things and don't deserve God's love.
We have been forgiven.
How great is our God!
We have told God we are sorry. We have been forgiven.
How great is our God!
We have decided to live God's way from now on. We have
been forgiven.
How great is our God!
God will forget about all our sins. We have been forgiven.
How great is our God!
He will go on loving us for ever. We have been forgiven.
How great is our God!
He will help us obey him. We have been forgiven.
How great is our God!
We want to become more like Jesus. We have been forgiven.
How great is our God!

Psalm 32 reassures us

Leader: Happy are those whose sins are forgiven.
All: Happy are those whose wrongs are pardoned.
Leader: When I did not confess my sins
All: I was worn out all day long.
Leader: Then I confessed my sins to you,
All: And you forgave them all.
Leader: Be glad and rejoice because of what the Lord has
done.
All: You that obey him, shout for joy!

Absolution

Invite everyone to go round putting the sign of the cross on
people's palms or foreheads, saying: 'Because of the cross,
we are forgiven.'

4
STATEMENTS OF BELIEF

What we believe

Teach the congregation this creed, which they should say and do together:

Christ had died, (*stretch arms wide in the shape of a cross*),
Christ is risen, (*hold open hands in front of you at chest level*),
Christ will come again, (*point upwards*).

As an alternative to actions, the congregation could clap rhythmically on the beat (Christ, died, Christ, ris. . . , Christ, come, . . .gain).

Having learnt it, invite the congregation to say it after each line:

Leader: We believe in God the Father, who created our
  world and sent Jesus to save it. We declare . . .
We believe in Jesus, God's only Son, who walked in our
  world, a human but perfect in every way. We declare . . .
We believe in the Holy Spirit, whom God sent to live in
  his people when Jesus returned to heaven. We declare . . .
This is the faith of the Christian church. We declare . . .

Believing in Jesus

Jesus was born in Bethlehem. People of God, do you believe this?
Yes, that's what we believe!

Jesus grew in a human family. People of God, do you believe this?
Yes, that's what we believe!

Jesus was a man, perfect in every way. People of God, do you believe this?
Yes, that's what we believe!

Jesus is God, from eternity to eternity. People of God, do you believe this?
Yes, that's what we believe!

Jesus died on a wooden cross. People of God, do you believe this?
Yes, that's what we believe!

Jesus rose again on the third day. People of God, do you believe this?
Yes, that's what we believe!

Jesus returned to the glory of heaven. People of God, do you believe this?
Yes, that's what we believe!

Jesus is coming back to reign forever. People of God, do you believe this?
Yes, that's what we believe!

Rejoicing

Ask the younger children to lead the congregation in this credal shout, culminating in a leap in the air on the final word:

We believe in God the Father,
We believe in God the Son,
We believe in God the Holy Spirit.
Let's all praise him, three in one,
Hooray!

Based on Romans 10:9

Leader: Do you confess that Jesus is Lord?
All: We confess that Jesus is Lord.
Leader: Do you believe that God raised him from the dead?
All: We believe that God raised him from the dead.
Leader: Do you believe that you will be saved?
All: We believe that we will be saved.

Our belief in the Trinity

Do you believe in God the Father, creator and sustainer of
the world?
God who made the universe,
Jesus Christ the risen one,
Holy Spirit, power of God,
Hallelujah! Three in one!
Do you believe in Jesus Christ, who died and rose to be the
Saviour of the world?
God who made the universe,
Jesus Christ the risen one,
Holy Spirit, power of God,
Hallelujah! Three in one!
Do you believe in the Holy Spirit, God at work as helper
and comforter in our world?
God who made the universe,
Jesus Christ the risen one,
Holy Spirit, power of God,
Hallelujah! Three in one!

Using John 11:25–27

Leader: Jesus said: I am the resurrection,
All: And I am the life,
Leader: Whoever believes in me,
All: Will live, even though he dies,
Leader: And whoever lives and believes in me,
All: Will never die.
Leader: Do you believe this?
All: Yes, Lord Jesus, we do believe.

Adoring the Trinity

Creator God, we believe you sent your Son into our world
as you promised you would.
We worship and adore you.
Lord Jesus, we believe you are the Messiah, the long-awaited
leader of your people.
We worship and adore you.
Lord Jesus, we believe you came to earth to show us how
to live peacefully and fairly.
We worship and adore you.
Lord Jesus, we believe you will return as king over a new
world where peace and fairness will be established for
ever.
We worship and adore you.
Holy Spirit, we believe you live among us to guide us in
the way of the Messiah.
We worship and adore you.

The only one

The congregation respond to the leader with the repeated
italic line, stressing 'believe':

Maker of heaven and earth, and everything in them
We believe, Lord Jesus, we believe you are,
Born as a human, but God in every way,
We believe, Lord Jesus, we believe you are,
Dead, but risen to life, never to die again,
We believe, Lord Jesus, we believe you are,
The only one who can forgive our sins,
We believe, Lord Jesus, we believe you are,
The only one worth devoting our lives to,
We believe, Lord Jesus, we believe you are,
With us now and our friend through all eternity,
We believe, Lord Jesus, we believe you are.

Based on Daniel 6:26–27

Leader: Everyone should fear and respect God.
All: He is a living God.
Leader: He will rule forever.
All: His kingdom will never be destroyed.
Leader: His power will never come to an end.
All: He saves and rescues.
Leader: He performs wonders,
All: And miracles in heaven and on earth.

Responsive creed

I believe in God the Father,
I believe in God the Son,
I believe in God the Holy Spirit.
The Father made the heavens and earth,
And every day, in spite
Of all the errors that we make,
It keeps on working right.
I believe in God the Father,
I believe in God the Son,
I believe in God the Holy Spirit.
The Son was Jesus – born like us
To live a human life,
He died and rose so we could find
A way out of our strife.
I believe in God the Father,
I believe in God the Son,
I believe in God the Holy Spirit.
The Holy Spirit comes inside,
To help us live God's way,
And makes sure God is recognised
Throughout the world today.
I believe in God the Father,
I believe in God the Son,
I believe in God the Holy Spirit.

5
ACTS OF
DEDICATION

Symbols of giving

Invite everyone, with their eyes shut, to clench their fists
tightly. Ask them to think about what difficulties and temptations will face them this week. While a piece of music plays,
they are to decide whether they are prepared to stay faithful
to Jesus through them all, whatever it costs. When and if
they feel ready to dedicate themselves to Jesus, they should
open their hands as a private sign that they have let go of
these things and given them to God in trust. As the music
moves to its end, the leader reads these words by
J W van Deventer:

All to Jesus I surrender,
All to him I freely give,
I will ever love and trust him,
In his presence daily live,
I surrender all, I surrender all,
All to you my blessed Saviour,
I surrender all.

Welcoming the light

The leader should read Isaiah 60:1–3,19–20. Every time the
word 'light' occurs, the congregation should shout joyfully:
'Shine, Jesus, shine'. You might suggest a hand action to
accompany this so that young children can join in. Follow
with an appropriate hymn.

Putting on Jesus' love

I am putting on the love of my Lord Jesus Christ,
I want to be made new.
I am putting on the new life he offers and I will never be
the same,
I want to be made new.
I am putting on the Holy Spirit who guarantees that no one
will steal me from the Lord.
I want to be made new.
By the love of the Saviour, poured endlessly on me since
the creation of the world,
I want to be made new.
By the power of the cross on which Christ died on my
behalf,
I want to be made new.
By the grace of his forgiveness, made certain because Christ
pleads for me in the presence of Almighty God,
I want to be made new.
I am putting off the old, I am putting on the new,
I want to be made new.

God's invitation

Lord God, you invite us to a party which is greater than
any party on earth. Lord, with gratitude,
I accept your invitation.
You invite us to come now and not delay for a moment.
Lord, with gratitude,
I accept your invitation.
You invite us to turn away from our sins in the knowledge
that you will forgive us. Lord, with gratitude,
I accept your invitation.
You invite us to start the party here, living in the joy and
obedience of following Jesus. Lord, with gratitude,
I accept your invitation.
You invite us to carry on the party in the endless happiness
of heaven. Lord, with gratitude,
I accept your invitation.
And we know that you will never turn away anyone who
wants to come to you. Lord, with gratitude,
I accept your invitation.

Based on Isaiah 43:1–5

The Lord who created you says,
Do not be afraid.
I have called you by name.
Do not be afraid.
Your troubles will not overwhelm you.
Do not be afraid.
The hard trials that come will not hurt you.
Do not be afraid.
Because you are precious to me,
Do not be afraid.
Because I love you and give you honour,
Do not be afraid.
I am with you.
Do not be afraid. Amen.

The good shepherd

Jesus is a loving shepherd,
We will follow him,
Jesus is a gentle shepherd,
We will follow him,
Jesus the protecting shepherd,
We will follow him,
Jesus the eternal shepherd,
We will follow him,
Life in all its fullness shepherd,
We will follow him,
Jesus Christ the Good Shepherd,
We will follow him.

Prayer of commitment

Invite the congregation thoughtfully to repeat each phrase:

Lord Jesus, I love you. . . .
Lord Jesus, thank you that you loved me first . . .
Lord Jesus, I'm sorry for the things I've done wrong . . .
Lord Jesus, I want to be different . . .
Lord Jesus, I want to be like you . . .
Lord Jesus, make me new . . . Amen.

RESOURCES

Voices, hands, feet, minds

Leader: We have voices to encourage, to praise and to
advise. We offer our voices to serve you, Lord.
All: We offer our voices to serve each other.
Leader: We have hands to carry, to touch and to work. We
offer our hands to serve you, Lord.
All: We offer our hands to serve each other.
Leader: We have feet to travel, to help and to bring good
news. We offer our feet to serve you, Lord.
All: We offer our feet to serve each other.
Leader: We have minds to learn, to respect and to care. We
offer our minds to serve you, Lord.
All: We offer our minds to serve each other.

Everything for God

Leader: Everything comes from you, Lord,
All: Everything comes from you,
Leader: All that I have is yours, Lord,
All: All that I have is yours,
Leader: Out of my love, I give, Lord,
All: Out of my love, I give,
Leader: Take what I offer you, Lord,
All: Take what I offer you,
Leader: All that I am I share, Lord,
All: All that I am I share,
Leader: I give all I have to you, Lord,
All: I give all I have to you.

God's friends

Ask everyone to think of a way to finish the sentence,
'Because God is my friend. . .'. (Suggest as examples:
'Because God is my friend, he will never let me down', or
more simply, 'Because God is my friend, I am happy'.) After
some time, invite them to call out their suggestions and write
them up. When seven or eight are listed, ask
a musician to play some music as members of the congregation choose and declare one, or the leader reads the list
worshipfully.

Offering our lives to God

Lord God, here are our lives,
Here they are, offered to you.
Given in sadness, given in gladness;
Given for the joy of living, given for the security of dying;
Given for determined service on earth, given for everlasting
  rest in heaven;
Given because you have loved us from the beginning, given
  because you will love us until the end;
You have the words of eternal life, and we will never die,
Lord God, here are our lives,
Here they are for now; here they are forever.

God with me

Teach young children the actions, so that they can join in
even if they are unable to read the words:

God is with me in the good times, (*thumbs up*),
When I'm happy so is he, (*smile*),
God is with me in the good times, (*thumbs up*),
That's because he cares for me, (*point to self*).
God is with me in the bad times, (*thumbs down*),
When I'm sad he won't let go, (*cross arms across chest*),
God is with me in the bad times, (*thumbs down*),
That's because he loves me so, (*point to self*).

Based on Hosea 2:19–23

Leader: God says, 'My precious people, I will take you as
my wife.'
All: You will be true and faithful.
Leader: God says, 'I will show you constant love and
mercy.'
All: We will be yours forever.
Leader: God says, 'I will keep my promise and make you
mine.'
All: We will acknowledge you as Lord.
Leader: God says, 'I will answer all your prayers.'
All: You show love to all who were unloved.
Leader: God says, 'You are indeed my people.'
All: And you are our God. Alleluia.

Using Psalm 23

God is with us wherever we go,
God is with us wherever we go.
God is with us in the peaceful places, when we wander
through green fields and by quiet waters,
God is with us wherever we go.
God is with us in difficult places, when we walk on high
paths or through dark valleys,
God is with us wherever we go.
God gives us new strength; he takes away our fears and
protects us from our enemies,
God is with us wherever we go.
God prepares good things for us; he teaches us how to enjoy
our time with him,
God is with us wherever we go.

Using 2 Timothy 2:11–13

Leader: If we have died with him,
All: We shall also live with him.
Leader: If we continue to endure,
All: We shall also rule with him.
Leader: If we deny him,
All: He will also deny us.
Leader: But even if we are not faithful,
All: He remains faithful.

Making Jesus welcome

Jesus, born in a borrowed room,
Make your home in my life.
Jesus, traveller through Judaea,
Make your home in my life.
Jesus, with nowhere to lie down and rest,
Make your home in my life.
Jesus, driven from some towns, welcomed in others,
Make your home in my life.
Jesus, laid in a borrowed tomb,
Make your home in my life.
Jesus, risen and ascended to heaven,
Make your home in my life.
Jesus, welcome as our friend and Lord,
Make your home in my life. Amen.

Never afraid

When the darkness closes in,
I need never be afraid,
When my nerves are wearing thin,
I need never be afraid,
When I walk a scary path,
I need never be afraid,
When there's spiders in the bath,
I need never be afraid,
When I face exams next day,
I need never be afraid,
When my home is far away,
I need never be afraid,
Then God says to me, 'Be strong,'
I need never be afraid,
'I am with you all day long,'
I need never be afraid,
'I have planned things perfectly,'
I need never be afraid,
'You can put your trust in me.'
I need never be afraid.

Based on Psalm 131

Lord God, I have given up my pride.
I simply put my trust in you.
I have turned away from my arrogant ways.
I simply put my trust in you.
I'm not thinking of all the complicated problems about you.
I simply put my trust in you.
I'm not fussed about things too hard for me to understand.
I simply put my trust in you.
Lord, I am content and at peace.
I simply put my trust in you.
You are a mother and I am a child in your arms.
I simply put my trust in you.
Let me be quiet in your loving presence.
I simply put my trust in you.
Trust in the Lord, now and forever.
I simply put my trust in you.

Christ's authority

Lord Jesus we acknowledge. . . .
That you have authority over the world,
We your followers bow before you,
That you have authority over your church,
We your followers bow before you,
That you have authority over each one of us,
We your followers bow before you,
That you will teach and we will obey,
We your followers bow before you,
That you will guide and we will go,
We your followers bow before you,
That you will decide and we will accept,
We your followers bow before you,
High above all creation, we praise your authority
We your followers bow before you.

God who answers prayer

Our God answers prayer today,
Nothing is too hard for God,
So with thanks and joy we say,
Nothing is too hard for God,
Power so great and love so deep,
Nothing is too hard for God,
Every promise he will keep,
Nothing is too hard for God,
Wants the best for you and me,
Nothing is too hard for God,
You can trust him totally,
Nothing is too hard for God,
No one takes his power away,
Nothing is too hard for God,
Don't forget it, night and day,
Nothing is too hard for God.

Based on Romans 8:35

The shouted responses grow louder and louder:

Leader: Who can separate us from the love of Christ?
All: Nothing can separate us from the love of Christ.
Leader: Can trouble do it?
All: No!
Leader: Can hardship do it?
All: No!
Leader: Can persecution do it?
All: No!
Leader: Can hunger do it?
All: No!
Leader: Can poverty do it?
All: No!
Leader: Can danger do it?
All: No!
Leader: Can death do it?
All: No!
Leader: So who can separate us from the love of Christ?
All: Nothing can separate us from the love of Christ.

Based on Proverbs 3:4–7

Leader: Trust in the Lord with all your heart.
All: We will.
Leader: Never rely just on what you think you know.
All: We won't.
Leader: Remember the Lord in everything you do.
All: We will.
Leader: Let God show you the right way.
All: We will.
Leader: Never let yourself think that you are wiser than you are.
All: We won't.
Leader: Simply obey the Lord and refuse to do wrong.
All: We will.
Leader: If you do this, both God and humans will be pleased with you.
All: That's what we want. Amen.

Turning from evil

All that would lead me toward evil,
I turn away from,
All that would lead me toward sadness,
I turn away from,
All that would lead me toward hatred,
I turn away from,
All that would lead me toward darkness,
I turn away from,
All that would lead me toward temptation,
I turn away from,
All that would lead me toward trouble,
I turn away from,
All that would lead me toward conflict,
I turn away from,
Keep me, Lord, as the apple of your eye,
Hide me under the shelter of your wing. Amen.

Based on Joshua 24:15

Choose for yourselves this day whom you will serve,
As for me and my people, we will serve the Lord.
Choose between a life serving Jesus and a life pleasing
  yourself,
As for me and my people, we will serve the Lord.
Choose between a life of obedience and a life of selfishness,
As for me and my people, we will serve the Lord.
Choose between rejecting Jesus and accepting him as Son
  of God,
As for me and my people, we will serve the Lord.
Choose between making Jesus first priority, and making
  him nothing at all,
As for me and my people, we will serve the Lord.
May God Almighty strengthen us to fulfil our choices,
As for me and my people, we will serve the Lord.

Offering myself

My talents and my practised skills,
All I shall be for you, Lord, all shall be for you,
My gifts and my qualifications,
All shall be for you, Lord, all shall be for you,
The praise for my achievements,
All shall be for you, Lord, all shall be for you,
The credit for my successes,
All shall be for you, Lord, all shall be for you,
The best of my creativity,
All shall be for you, Lord, all shall be for you,
The richness of my imagination,
All shall be for you, Lord, all shall be for you,
The lessons I learn from my failures,
All shall be for you, Lord, all shall be for you,
The whole of my life transformed by your Holy Spirit,
All shall be for you, Lord, all shall be for you.

Acknowledging need

In growing and developing, our children need Jesus,
Lord Jesus, we need you.
In deciding and standing firm, our teenagers need Jesus,
Lord Jesus, we need you.
In choosing and persevering, our adults need Jesus,
Lord Jesus, we need you.
In serving and directing, our leaders need Jesus,
Lord Jesus, we need you.
In welcoming and being an example, our church needs Jesus,
Lord Jesus, we need you.
In caring and bringing justice, our nation needs Jesus,
Lord Jesus, we need you.
In co-operating and surviving, our world needs Jesus,
Lord Jesus, we need you.
In every country and every place, everyone needs Jesus,
Lord Jesus, we need you. Amen.

Following Jesus

Jesus, we have heard you call us,
Lord, we want to follow you,
And whatever may befall us,
Lord, we want to follow you,
Like the fishermen who met you,
Lord, we want to follow you,
We will worship, not forget you,
Lord, we want to follow you,
Introducing you to others,
Lord, we want to follow you,
Just like Andrew with his brothers,
Lord, we want to follow you,
All our deepest needs supplying,
Lord, we want to follow you,
Even when it's tough and trying,
Lord, we want to follow you.

Based on 2 Corinthians 4:7–15

Leader: Sometimes we feel as feeble as pots of clay,
All: But we have God's power within us.
Leader: We are often in trouble,
All: But we are not crushed,
Leader: We are sometimes in doubt,
All: But we are never in despair,
Leader: We may have many enemies,
All: But we are never without a friend,
Leader: We are badly hurt at times,
All: But we cannot be destroyed.
Leader: God's grace reaches more and more people,
All: And we will give glory to God.

Using 1 Chronicles 29:11–13

Leader: You, Lord, are great and powerful, glorious,
  splendid and majestic,
All: Everything in heaven and earth is yours.
Leader: All money and possessions come from you,
All: And we give you what is already your own.
Leader: Now, our God, we give you thanks,
All: And praise your glorious name.

At an offertory

Lord, you've given us so much,
Now we give this back to you,
Precious sights and sounds and touch,
Now we give this back to you,
Others who can be a friend,
Now we give this back to you,
Sometimes money we can spend,
Now we give this back to you,
In return these gifts seem small,
Now we give this back to you,
They're a present from us all,
Now we give this back to you,
Here and now we want to state,
Now we give this back to you,
Thank you, Lord, you're really great,
Now we give this back to you.

Giving God our gifts

Leader: Lord Jesus, you love us so much that you entered our world to share our joys and sorrows. Lord,
All: Receive the gift of our love.
Leader: Because of your death and resurrection, we share eternal life with you. Lord,
All: Receive the gift of our lives.
Leader: You came as a servant to show us how we must care for others. Lord,
All: Receive the gift of our service.
Leader: You have given us much, and want us to share what we have with those in need. Lord,
All: Receive the gift of our money.
Leader: You long for us to praise you, and we want to make you glad. Lord,
All: Receive the gift of our worship. Amen.

Offertory

As a symbol of unity and trust, vary the presentation of the offertory by forming a chain of people of all ages and passing it from one to another to the front of the room.

6
PRAYERS OF INTERCESSION

For peace in the world

Pray for places in the world where there is currently potential for violence. Mention the places by name and after each, use this response:

Leader: Lord, before people reach for weapons,
All: Incline their hearts to peace.

For weapons to be dismantled

Ask the congregation to call out the names of all the weapons mankind has invented, from fists to bombs. As they are mentioned, write up a list for all to see. Include less obvious 'weapons' such as aggressive words. The leader should read Revelation 21:3–4, then say this responsive prayer several times, inserting one or more
of the weapons in the gap:

Leader: We look forward to the time when . . . no longer exist.
All: Give us peace on earth.

For the Holy Spirit to transform our town

Read Luke 4:18–19 one phrase at a time. After each phrase, use this response:

Leader: Spirit of the Lord, come down,
All: Fulfil these words throughout our town.

Ready to serve God

Jesus came among us not to give orders, but to be a servant. Following this example, we pray . . .
Make us ready to serve you, Lord.
Our world needs to hear about Jesus as urgently now as then. We pray . . .
Make us ready to serve you, Lord.
Still Jesus needs people to bring love and peace between parents and children. We pray . . .
Make us ready to serve you, Lord.
Stil Jesus needs people to turn the disobedient back to God's way. We pray . . .
Make us ready to serve you, Lord.
Jesus is coming again soon. Looking forward to that day, we pray . . .
Make us ready to serve you, Lord.

For national leaders

Pray for the national leaders of the world, beginning with the Prime Minister of your own country and extending your prayers worldwide. Use this pattern:

A: We pray for . . . , the Prime Minister of . . . ,
B: (*Reads a sentence from a newspaper related to the present concerns and responsibilities of that person*).
A: Make your chosen leader wise and just.
B: Your will be done on earth as in heaven.

For the world's injustice

In order to pray for areas in the world where injustice, corruption and oppression are rife, cut headlines and photographs from this week's newspapers and paste them on to white sheets of paper. Photocopy these on to acetate (you will need special acetates for this, but any high street copy shop should be able to help you). Display them using an overhead projector as you mention each one in prayer, or leave a space after each picture is shown for spontaneous or silent prayers.

Blessing the locality

I call to mind those I shall meet,
Send your blessing Lord on these,
Those passed in silence in my street,
Send your blessing Lord on these,
Those far too rushed to say hello,
Send your blessing Lord on these,
And those whose names I do not know,
Send your blessing Lord on these,
Those who've been cruel to me before,
Send your blessing Lord on these,
And those who cry behind their door,
Send your blessing Lord on these,
I pray, Lord for my neighbourhood,
Send your blessing Lord on these,
Bless it with every kind of good,
Send your blessing Lord on these. Amen.

'Spies' in the neighbourhood

At the beginning of a service, send out three groups of 'spies', reflecting the actions of the spies whom Moses sent out into the land in Numbers 13. They could be a family, a group of teenagers, a mixed group of adults and children, or any other combination of people who have agreed to contribute to the service in this way. Send each one to a specific location – a nearby park, a row of shops, a street corner, and so on. Ask them to 'spy out' what is going on in the neighbourhood of the church and identify things for which the church needs to pray (for example, an elderly lady has been taken ill in the high street, there is a group of bored teenagers hanging around by the pub, a brother and sister are having a row in the park, there are shops open which should be closed on a Sunday, and so on). When they arrive back at a specified time, they should report to the church what they have noticed, and this should immediately be followed by a time of prayer for all that is happening at that moment in the surrounding area.

For countries where there is violence or evil

Leader: Into the darkness of Bosnia, Lord, may your light shine.
All: Fill the land with your glory.
Leader: Into the darkness of Somalia, Lord, may your light shine.
All: Fill the land with your glory.

Continue with other nations, concluding with this response, and any appropriate hymn:

Leader: Wherever there is darkness in this land, Lord, may your light shine.
All: Fill the land with your glory.

For missionaries

Focus on missionaries linked with your church – those abroad, those who are at work on evangelism schemes in your own area, those who witness as part of their day-to-day conversation. Finish each prayer with this response:

Leader: These, Lord, are your witnesses.
All: Help them tell others about you.

For mission at home

Focus on your own church as a centre for spreading good news. Draw attention to any visiting or evangelism scheme that is run, literature that is distributed, 'drop-in' centre, playgroup, holiday club and so on. Invite the leaders to stand so that they can more readily be recognised. Some could report, in a sentence, on their work. Conclude with prayers, adding specific names and details to this responsive prayer:

Leader: We pray for the work of . . . , Lord, as the good news goes out,
All: May your name be glorified.

For church leaders

> **Leader:** We pray for the church throughout the world. For missionaries, especially . . .
> **All:** We pray for the church throughout the world.
> **Leader:** For Chrsitians in countries where Sunday is not a day of rest.
> **All:** We pray for the church throughout the world.
> **Leader:** For Christians persecuted because of their faith.
> **All:** We pray for the church throughout the world.
> **Leader:** We pray for the church in this country. For its leaders, especially . . .
> **All:** We pray for the church in this country.
> **Leader:** For the different churches working together in this town (city, village).
> **All:** We pray for the church in this country.
> **Leader:** For Christians who speak out about justice and morality.
> **All:** We pray for the church in this country.
> **Leader:** We pray for this church where we worship. For our leaders, especially . . .
> **All:** We pray for this church where we worship.
> **Leader:** For those in need today, especially . . .
> **All:** We pray for this church where we worship.
> **Leader:** For all of us, as we spread the good news about Jesus.
> **All:** We pray for this church where we worship.

For the future of the church

Pray for God's direction in the future of your church; for new revelations of God's power; for willingness to be open to God's leading; for all who live in fear; for God to be recognised in the mundane places we will visit this week. After each prayer, use the words of Genesis 28:15,21:

Leader: God says, 'I will not leave you until I have done all I promise.'
All: He will be my God.

For the nation's protection

Based on Isaiah 8:8–10.

Almighty Father, protect this nation from evil. God is with us.
His outspread wings protect the land.
Protect this nation from war. God is with us.
His outspread wings protect the land.
Protect this nation from injustice. God is with us.
His outspread wings protect the land.
Protect this nation from all who seek to turn people away from you. God is with us.
His outspread wings protect the land.
Protect this nation from those who want to lower moral standards. God is with us.
His outspread wings protect the land.
Those who plan to defy God will never succeed. They may talk as much as they like, but it is useless. God is with us.
His outspread wings protect the land.

For protection of those we know

In advance, prepare an acetate for the overhead projector with the words: 'The angel of the Lord encamps around those who honour him', written in a circle, with an empty space in the centre. Teach the congregation the words, which come from Psalm 34:7, and comment on how rich is the image of being totally surrounded by God's protection, as if he had set up camp all around. Go on to pray for particular members of the congregation who face a worrying future for any reason. One at a time, display their names on an overhead projector. Instead of saying, 'Amen', overlay the circular acetate and say the verse, imagining God encircling the person as certainly as the words do.

Prayers for those newly married

Pray for all those in the congregation who have married during the past year (or anyone who has used the building for their wedding). Do this by borrowing slides of the wedding day from the families of the couples (or transferring photographs on to acetate) and showing them to the background of a piece of music traditionally played at weddings (eg, *The Wedding March*, Mendelssohn; *A Whiter Shade of Pale*, Procul Harem). Follow this by praying for them by name, asking for them to grow in love and understanding, both in good times and bad. (As a means of outreach, you might invite recently married couples to come to church and take part in these prayers).

For the life of the church

Using the themes of Philippians 2, pray for the unity, care and example of your own congregation:

Lord God, may this church be full of kindness and
compassion. So that all may give glory to God,
Make us more like Jesus.
May this church be humble, looking out for one another's
interests. So that all may give glory to God,
Make us more like Jesus.
May this church be willing and able to obey God's purpose.
So that all may give glory to God,
Make us more like Jesus.
May this church hold out a message of life. So that all may
give glory to God,
Make us more like Jesus.
May this church be glad and full of joy. So that all may
give glory to God,
Make us more like Jesus.

Using the names of Jesus

Leader: Jesus the Christ,
All: Have mercy upon us.
Leader: Jesus the Teacher,
All: Guide us.
Leader: Jesus the Healer,
All: Heal us.
Leader: Jesus, Son of Man,
All: Help us.
Leader: Jesus the King,
All: Rule in our hearts.
Leader: Jesus the Anointed One,
All: Make us more like you. Amen.

For groups in the church

Pray for all the groups which together serve the church. The leader should name them one at a time, using Philippians 1:9 as a repeated prayer, thus:

Leader: Lord God, we pray for *the Brownies*. This is our prayer,
All: That their love keeps growing more and more.
Leader: Lord God, we pray for *the choir*. This is our prayer,
All: That their love keeps growing more and more.
Leader: Lord God, we pray for the *drop-in centre*. This is our prayer . . .

Conclude with the words of Philippians 1:11, 'May our lives be filled with the truly good qualities that only Jesus can produce for the glory and praise of God.'

For the Spirit to fill our lives

Invite the congregation to talk together in small groups about how they would complete the prayer: 'Holy Spirit, come into our lives to. . .'. After a minute, ask them to call out their suggestions and make a list of them. The leader should then turn their suggestions into a prayer, or introduce a time of open prayer which reflects those themes.

For the Spirit to change us

Leader: O God, we want to see clearly what would please you,
All: Give us the Holy Spirit's light.
Leader: We want to have strength to do what is right,
All: Give us the Holy Spirit's power.
Leader: We want to live in peace with those who do not share our faith,
All: Give us the Holy Spirit's love.
Leader: We want to talk to them about you with confidence,
All: Give us the Holy Spirit's wisdom.
Leader: We want others to see what a difference you make to our lives,
All: Give us the Holy Spirit's joy. Amen.

For a love like Jesus' love

Pharisees and wicked men,
Jesus loves them all,
Saints and sinners, now and then,
Jesus loves them all,
Every country, everywhere,
Jesus loves them all,
People no one else can bear,
Jesus loves them all,
Every type of hair or skin,
Jesus loves them all,
Short or giant, thick or thin,
Jesus loves them all,
Good at school or with a ball,
Jesus loves them all,
Good at nothing much at all,
Jesus loves them all,
Poor or rich, between the two,
Jesus loves them all,
Help us love them just like you,
Jesus loves them all. Amen.

For lives without prejudice

Father of all, you are the loving and merciful God, always
patient and always kind. But we know we don't always
treat others the way you want us to. We think of people
we hurt or keep away from because they are different
from us. Lord God, change us,
And teach us how to love them.
People who feel unwelcome in our church because of our
attitude to them. Lord God, change us,
And teach us how to love them.
People we are wary of because of the way they speak or
look or dress. Lord God, change us,
And teach us how to love them.
People who are scorned in newspapers because of the
country they come from, the colour of their skin, the
way they live their lives or the company they keep. Lord
God, change us,
And teach us how to love them.

For temptation to be overcome

When I'm tempted to do wrong,
Lord, don't let me let you down,
Hurt someone to prove I'm strong,
Lord, don't let me let you down,
Pick on someone who is weak,
Lord, don't let me let you down,
Answer back with cruel cheek,
Lord, don't let me let you down,
Dodge from touble with a lie,
Lord, don't let me let you down,
Steal something I ought to buy,
Lord, don't let me let you down,
Jesus, you were tempted too,
Lord, don't let me let you down,
Make me strong and firm as you,
Lord, don't let me let you down.

Based on Mark 10:46–52

Leader: Jesus is very close to us at this moment.
All: Jesus, take pity on us.
Leader: Cheer up! He is calling to us!
All: Jesus, take pity on us.
Leader: He asks, 'What do you want me to do for you?'
Silence for people to make silent or spoken pleas to Jesus.
Leader: Jesus declares, 'Go, your faith has made you well.'
All: Amen. Jesus, we will follow you.

For the Holy Spirit to fill the church

Leader: Prince of Peace, when we are in disagreement,
All: May your Spirit unite us.
Leader: When we are angry with each other,
All: May your Spirit make us gentle.
Leader: When we meet together and at all times,
All: May your Spirit lead us to rejoice.
Leader: When we are worried or anxious,
All: May your Spirit fill us with peace. Amen.

For the help of the Trinity

Leader: Lord God, in sickness heal us,
All: Jesus, in sickness heal us,
Spirit, in sickness heal us.
Leader: Lord God, in stress calm us,
All: Jesus, in stress calm us,
Spirit, in stress calm us.
Leader: Lord God, in tiredness rest us,
All: Jesus, in tiredness rest us,
Spirit, in tiredness rest us.
Leader: Lord God, in danger protect us,
All: Jesus, in danger protect us,
Spirit, in danger protect us.
Leader: Lord God, in weakness strengthen us,
All: Jesus, in weakness strengthen us,
Spirit, in weakness strengthen us.
Leader: Lord God, in death welcome us,
All: Jesus, in death welcome us,
Spirit, in death welcome us.
Leader: Lord, surround us, Jesus, fulfil us, Spirit, uphold
us, Trinity of God, give us your peace. Amen.

Based on Acts 4:24–30

Leader: Master of heaven,
All: Creator of the earth and seas,
Leader: Speak through your Holy Spirit,
All: As you spoke to your servants of old.
Leader: Allow us to proclaim your message,
All: Allow us to speak with boldness,
Leader: Stretch out your hand to heal,
All: Grant that wonders may be performed.
Leader: Through the name of your servant Jesus,
All: Shake us again with the power of your Spirit.

For help in trouble

It is hard to know what to say when we are accused of something we have not done. Loving God, in times of trouble,
Hear us and help us. Amen.
It is hard to be patient when things are obviously not fair. Loving God, in times of trouble,
Hear us and help us. Amen.
It is hard to resist when we are tempted to do wrong. Loving God, in times of trouble,
Hear us and help us. Amen.
It is hard to stay calm when we have the opportunity to get our own back. Loving God, in times of trouble,
Hear us and help us. Amen.
It is hard to stay faithful when people have neglected or forgotten about us. Loving God, in times of trouble,
Hear us and help us. Amen.
We pray for all those we know for whom life is not easy at present. Loving God, in times of trouble.
Hear us and help us. Amen.

Perseverance

When difficulties face us,
Help us, Lord, to keep following.
When temptations distract us,
Help us, Lord, to keep following.
When failures discourage us,
Help us, Lord, to keep following.
When tragedy makes us doubt,
Help us, Lord, to keep following.
When opposition makes us fearful,
Help us, Lord, to keep following.
When tiredness makes us feel like giving up,
Help us, Lord, to keep following.
Until we reach the perfect joy of heaven,
Help us, Lord, to keep following. Amen.

For our spiritual lives

With thanks I pray to you, Lord,
With thanks I pray to you.
With praise I pray to you, Lord,
With praise I pray to you.
With hope I pray to you, Lord,
With hope I pray to you.
It's right to pray to you, Lord,
It's right to pray to you.
It's good to pray to you, Lord,
It's good to pray to you.
It's hard to pray to you, Lord,
It's hard to pray to you.
For trust we pray to you, Lord,
For trust we pray to you.
For health we pray to you, Lord,
For health we pray to you.
For peace we pray to you, Lord,
For peace we pray to you.

Based on St Anselm's prayer

We bring before you, O Lord, the griefs and perils of people and nations. O merciful Father . . .
Comfort and relieve them.
The necessities of the homeless. O merciful Father . . .
Comfort and relieve them.
The helplessness of the aged and weak. O merciful Father . . .
Comfort and relieve them.
The sighings of prisoners. O merciful Father . . .
Comfort and relieve them.
The pains of the sick and injured. O merciful Father . . .
Comfort and relieve them.
Comfort and relieve them according to their needs, for the sake of your Son, our Saviour Jesus Christ. Amen.

Based on St Francis' prayer

Leader: Make us channels of your peace. Where there is hatred,
All: Let us bring love.
Leader: Where there is injury,
All: Let us bring pardon.
Leader: Where there is doubt,
All: Let us bring faith.
Leader: Where there is despair,
All: Let us bring hope.
Leader: Where there is darkness,
All: Let us bring light.
Leader: Where there is sadness,
All: Let us bring joy. Amen.

For those who are sick

Draw around a hand on an overhead projector acetate and display the image. Ask members of the congregation to call out the names of people they know who are sick, needy or in distress. Write their names inside the outline. The leader should read Luke 4:40, then say a prayer which recognises Jesus' authority over illness of every kind and asks him to heal.

For families

Invite the congregation to picture in their minds a family (not their own) for whom they have a love and concern. Remind everyone of the deep care that Jesus has for that family. Invite them, in silence, to imagine that Jesus comes to visit them. Introduce each member of the family in turn to Jesus. After the silence, the leader should say a prayer for all families – those who live together happily, those where children have grown up and left home, those who are spread out across the country, those who feel hurt and under pressure, those who have something to celebrate, those who live alone and have friends as part of their extended family. After each category is mentioned, use this response:

Leader: Jesus, these are your brothers and sisters.
All: We are one family in you.

For those who suffer

In each line of the prayer, particular names of people known to the congregation could be included by adding: 'Especially. . .'.

Saviour God, we pray for those who are sick. We lift them up to you, Lord.
Hold them and heal them, we pray.
We pray for those who are mourning the death of people they love. We lift them up to you, Lord.
Hold them and heal them, we pray.
We pray for those who are homeless, hungry or helplessly poor. We lift them up to you, Lord.
Hold them and heal them, we pray.
We pray for those who are lonely or unloved. We lift them up to you, Lord.
Hold them and heal them, we pray.
We pray for those who suffer because they spread the good news about Jesus. We lift them up to you Lord.
Hold them and heal them, we pray.
We pray for those who don't know where to turn for help. We lift them up to you, Lord.
Hold them and heal them, we pray.

Mentioning the needy

Divide this prayer between three or more voices, with reflective silences:

Holy God, three in one, we lift to you those in need,
The hungry, the homeless, the helpless,
The bullied, the betrayed, the bereaved,
The sick, the silly, the sad,
The disabled, the disturbed, the deceived,
The anxious, the abused, the addicted,
The imprisoned, the ignored, the isolated,
Holy God, three in one, hear our prayer for those in need.
  Amen.

Prayer of contrasts

A: O God who hears, we pray for those who long to make friends,
B: And those who long to be alone.
A: Those who are desperate to grow up,
B: And those afraid of growing old.
A: Those who long for someone close,
B: And those whose partner brings them pain.
A: Those who long for their own children,
B: And those who are not pleased to be pregnant.
A: Those confined to their homes,
B: And those who have no home at all.
A: Those who hate being unemployed,
B: And those who have far too much to do.
A: Those who have no world but church,
B: And those who have no time for God.

7
BEGINNINGS AND ENDINGS

Beginnings

Preparing to praise

God has called us here this morning,
All the world give God your praises,
Let us offer him our worship,
All the world give God your praises,
Let us thank him for his goodness,
All the world give God your praises,
Let us ask him to forgive us,
All the world give God your praises,
Let us learn what he would teach us,
All the world give God your praises,
Let us bring our prayers before him,
All the world give God your praises.

Preparing to meet Jesus

Leader: We will meet Jesus,
All: And we will worship Jesus.
Leader: We will pray to Jesus,
All: And we will learn from Jesus.
Leader: We will praise Jesus,
All: Alleluia! Praise him!

Call to worship

Leader: God rejoices when we come together to worship him. So we have gathered as his family, knowing he is with us, and we will give him praise.
All: Help us, Lord, to praise you.
Leader: We will hear what he wants to teach us through the Bible.
All: Help us, Lord, to learn from you.
Leader: We will pray to him about the needs of the world.
All: Help us, Lord, to pray to you.
Leader: We will ask him to forgive us our sins.
All: Help us, Lord, to be truly sorry.
Leader: We will enjoy the friendship of our brothers and sisters in Christ.
All: Help us, Lord, to love each other. Amen.

Procession

As the service begins, play or sing a piece of music that celebrates the Lordship of God over the whole world. During this, an adult should place a globe on a table at the front of the room. A procession of children, teenagers and adults then each bring a lighted candle and place it on the table, completely surrounding the globe with flames of light.

Using Psalm 122:1

Leader: 'I was glad when they said to me: 'Let us go to the house of the Lord'. Words like these were used at the beginning of worship in Old Testament times. Were you thinking that as you left your home to come to church? Turn round to face the entrance and pretend to look back to the place you came from this morning . . .
Deliberately leave behind any worries you have about tasks left undone, any worries about people you left behind, any worries about disagreements unresolved, any worries about the lunch you will have later . . . Leave them behind and turn to face the front again. Now say after me, 'I was glad when they said to me: 'Let us go to the house of the Lord' . . .

Using Luke 2:14

Begin the service by teaching the congregation the words and actions of this acclamation:

Glory to God in the highest (*raise hands in the air*),
And peace to his people on earth (*shake hands with those sitting nearby*).

Rhythmic introduction

This call to worship is spoken together rhythmically, with a slow-paced finger click on the beat (we, family, God, Father, meet, here, give, etc):

Now we are the family of God,
Our Father will meet with us here,
To give him our praise and our thanks,
To hear and to learn from his word,
To bring him the needs of the world,
To ask his forgiveness for sin,
To look for the grace of his Son,
To give of ourselves as we serve.

Endings

Using the closing words of the Bible

Leader: Jesus says, 'Yes indeed! I am coming soon!'
All: So be it. Come, Lord Jesus.
Leader: May the love of the Lord Jesus be with everyone.
All: Amen! Amen!

Looking outward

Instead of concluding the service with everyone in their seats, invite the congregation to gather outside the doors of the building or by the windows where they can view the neighbourhood. Say a prayer asking God's blessing on the community. Invite the congregation to look outward as they say the words of 2 Corinthians 13:13.

Words of grace and peace

Based on Ephesians 1:2–3; 6:23–24:

Leader: May God our Father and the Lord Jesus Christ give you grace and peace.
All: Let us give thanks to the God and Father of our Lord Jesus Christ!
Leader: May God the Father and the Lord Jesus Christ give to all Christians peace and love with faith.
All: May God's grace be with all those who love Jesus with undying love. Amen.

Choosing to serve

Invite the congregation to review the ways God has challenged them during the service and silently commit themselves to the future, much as Joshua did (24:14–15), then declare:

Leader: Choose for yourselves today whom you will serve.
All: As for my family and me, we will serve the Lord.

Based on Isaiah 6:8

Jesus bids us, 'Go and make disciples.' Whom shall I send and who will go for us?
Here am I. Send me.
Jesus commands, 'Tell those who have never heard that I am alive.' Whom shall I send and who will go for us?
Here am I. Send me.
Jesus says, 'I speak to the world through your words.' Whom shall I send and who will go for us?
Here am I. Send me.
Jesus says, 'I care for the world through your hands.' Whom shall I send and who will go for us?
Here am I. Send me.
Jesus says, 'The harvest is plentiful, but the workers are few.' Whom shall I send and who will go for us?
Here am I. Send me.

Remembering those sent out

As people leave, give them a postcard which is blank on one side and pre-printed on the other with the address of a particular missionary and information about the cost of a stamp to reach that address. Encourage families and individuals to send a message when they get home, even if they do not know the missionary in person.

Going and telling

As everyone leaves, give them a self-adhesive address label on which is a speech balloon containing the words: 'Jesus is alive.' Invite them to wear it as a badge today, part of their own witness. Helium-filled balloons with a similar message would have an even greater impact.

8
CREATIVE ACTS OF WORSHIP

Worship using simple art

Family tree

Display a large cut-out tree on one of the walls. On large leaves, cut from green paper, write the names of those who are considered part of the local church family but are rarely seen because they are housebound, overseas on mission, doing shiftwork, working in the creche or another activity which occupies them during services, or perhaps have recently died. Mention each one individually in an appropriate prayer and, as you do so, attach the leaves (and photographs if possible) to the trees.

Growing up with God

Give everyone a piece of paper and a pencil. Invite those under forty to draw what they think they will look like in thirty years time, and those over forty to draw what they looked like thirty years ago. When they have done this they should find someone in the opposite group and compare their drawings. Recall God's promise that he is with us, working out his plan at every stage of our lives. Read Isaiah 43:1–3a, then praise God that he knows our pasts and our futures and that we are completely safe
with him.

An offering to God

Give each member of the congregation, young and old alike, a square of coloured paper. They fold it in half, then in half again (into a square), then across a diagonal (into a triangle). They tear holes from the edges, as illustrated, and open it out into a beautiful pattern. Ask them to show each other their results, and to put the scraps of paper in their pockets! Then take an offering, in which they may give their artwork to God. When the papers have been collected, the leader should lift them before God with a dedicatory prayer. A few families may like to spend the afternoon arranging the squares in a patchwork pattern on a wall of the room, a communal piece of creativity by the church for God.

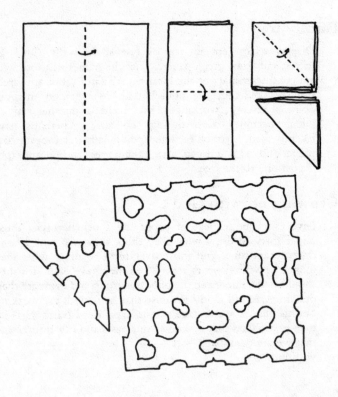

Prayers for the future

Give everyone a piece of paper and a pencil. Invite them to divide the paper into three sections by folding. In one section, they should draw what they will be doing at this time tomorrow; in the next section, something they are particularly looking forward to; in the last section, something they are not looking forward to. Give everyone a chance to tell their neighbours what their drawings mean. Remind the congregation that the risen Jesus will be with them in all these events. Say a three-part prayer with silences during which they can think about each drawing in turn.

Illustrating Psalm 8

On one wall of the room, display a huge piece of paper. On it are already drawn a sun and a moon. Invite any who are old enough to grasp a pen but too young to read to go to it, with a grown-up. They are each to draw a star on the picture of the sky. (It may be possible to do this with an overhead projector instead.) Meanwhile, those who are older sing a hymn. Thank the children for their contribution to your worship, and ask them to listen out for what they have drawn as Psalm 8 is read:

Leader: O Lord, our Lord, your greatness is seen in all the world!
Adults: Your praise reaches up to the heavens;
Children: It is sung by children and babies.
Leader: You are safe and secure from all your enemies;
Adults: You stop anyone who opposes you.
Children: I look at the sky, which you have made,
Leader: And at the moon and stars, which you set in their places.
Adults: Then I ask myself, what is it about humans that makes you even think of us?
Children: What is it about children that makes you love us?
Leader: Yet you made us inferior only to yourself; you crowned humankind with glory and honour.
Adults: You appointed us as rulers over everything you made.
Children: You made us the best of all the things you made.
All: Hosanna! Alleluia!

Fishers of men and women

Explain again what Jesus meant when he said that his followers would be 'fishing' for people. Give each member of the congregation a piece of paper in the shape of a fish, using as many colours as possible. Invite them to write on the shape the name of a person whom they would like to become a friend of Jesus. If they do not wish to write a name, they can draw a representative human shape or write 'my neighbour' or something similar. Ask one person in each row to collect the fish and bring them to the front, where the leader prays that these people will be introduced to Jesus. A couple of families may like to spend the afternoon arranging the shapes in a net hung on the wall of the building, under the heading, 'Jesus said, "Follow me and I will teach you how to fish for people." '

Go and make disciples

Ask the children to come to the front of the room. They are to draw around their feet on paper with felt pens. Arrange the footprints in a line down the centre of the room so that they form a symbolic pathway leading out of the church building into the world – a path which challenges all to follow as they leave the service. While the children are drawing, adults could sing songs which would otherwise be beyond the comprehension of children. Depending on the time and equipment available, children could draw one foot or both, cut out the shapes or leave them as outlines on paper, keep their shoes on or include their toes, add the words, 'Go, teach, make disciples', and so on.

Prayers for peace

Give everyone a piece of aluminium foil, about ten centimetres square, and ask them to mould the foil into a sword. Read Micah 4:3, then ask the congregation to remould their swords into something else – anything that would be useful to humans. When they have done this, they should show those sitting around them what they chose to make. The leader follows this with a prayer. What has been done symbolically will become a reality in Heaven.

Everyone a witness

On a wall display a large, simple outline of the building in which you meet. Give everyone a small slip of paper on which to write their names or draw themselves. While adults are singing appropriate songs, children collect the papers and put them inside the outline, attaching them with *Blu-tack*. Draw attention to the fact that everyone in the church is called to be a missionary – to those in their streets, at work or at school. Complete the display by drawing arrows heading outward from the building. Commit the congregation to mission in prayer: 'Lord God, in our conversations may you be mentioned, in our actions, may you be recognised, in our friendships may your love shine through. Amen.'

Flower festival

Over four weeks, ask someone to make flower arrangements that represent in some way a small aspect of the characters of God the Father, Jesus, the Spirit, and the Trinity. Each week, draw attention to the arrangement and ask its creator briefly to explain what they have tried to depict.

Reporters

At the beginning of the service, display a blank chart with the words, 'God's world . . .' on the left and '. . . spoiled' on the right. Give a Polaroid instant camera to a group consisting of one family and one single person (warn them in advance). Tell them that their contribution to the worship today is to take the camera into the surrounding area and photograph scenes which remind them of how beautiful God's world is and others which show how humans have failed to care for it. They are to return by a specified time to present the completed chart to the congregation – and to God. Display it after the service for people to examine in more detail. Encourage other families and groups to do the same later at home, and to display their own charts in the church building when the photographs have been developed.

Working for God

Give each person in the congregation a piece of paper about the size of a postcard. Ask them to tear from it the shape of a person and to write their own name on the shape. While adults are singing hymns which would otherwise be too complex for children to appreciate, ask those under about twelve to collect the paper people and hang them with paper-clips from a string the length of the room. Over it, display the caption, 'God's team, working together in (*your area*). Follow this with a time of prayer committing yourselves to God's service.

Praising God for his creation

Invite the congregation to form groups of six to nine people, or whatever size the seating comfortably allows. Each group needs paper and a pencil. It will help them to have a Bible open at Genesis 1. Ask one person from each group to come to the front – neither the youngest nor the oldest. Whisper to them one of the things that God created. They must return to the group and draw it. The person who guesses what it is comes to the front, to be told the next object to draw, and so on. The first drawing is of the sun; subsequently tell the representatives to draw birds, fruit trees, women, sea monsters, wild animals, men, fish, the moon. (If there is a congregation of several hundred, four or five leaders will be needed.) When about two-thirds of the groups have finished, stop the game and lead straight into a prayer thanking God for all the elements of creation mentioned in Genesis 1, or a similar time of open, spontaneous thanksgiving.

Thanksgiving for food

Invite the congregation to turn so as to make groups of three or four, adults and children together. Give each group a paper plate and ask them to draw (or write) on it the food that each person in the group would most like to thank God for. These can be brought to the front of the room and displayed on the wall under an appropriate heading. Follow with prayers that take up the same theme.

Praising God's power

Read Acts 3:1–8, then display a large copy of the leaping figure of the healed man. Invite the congregation to cluster into groups of two or three, children and adults together, and give each a pencil and a self-adhesive address label. Invite them to talk about this question: 'We know that the healed man praised God joyfully – what do you think he shouted out to God?' Give a minute or two for the groups to talk, then ask them to write their suggestion in a speech bubble on the label. While music plays, one from each group should post them around the figure. The leader should say a prayer which includes these words of praise, then invite everyone to look more closely after the service.

Shouts of Praise to God

Acts 3 :1-8

A cloud of praise

Give everyone a circular, plate-sized piece of paper in a bright colour. (These are available from craft shops, but hand-cut pieces of paper are suitable, no matter how inexact.) Ask them to gather into groups of three or four and talk together about words that describe how great Jesus is, or praise him for what he has done. While this is going on, display a life-size silhouette of Jesus cut from white paper or shiny foil, on a wall of the room. Ask everyone to write on the pieces of paper the words or phrases they are thinking of. Children too young to write should draw some shapes and squiggles in praise of Jesus instead. While songs of praise are being sung, collect the shapes and ask a group (of teenagers?) to arrange them, overlapping each other in a large cloud over the head of the silhouette. When this is done, the leader should read Matthew 17:1–5, and commit the words and shapes of praise to Jesus.

Starry praise

Give everyone in the congregation a piece of aluminium foil. Invite them to mould the foil into the shape of a star. While adults are singing hymns, those under about twelve should collect the stars up and bring them to the front where they can be attached to a sheet of black paper with *Blu-tack*. The resulting poster could be displayed with the words, 'Shine like stars in the sky', from Philippians 2:15. Pray for all Christians who try to be 'lights' where there is moral darkness.

Newspaper prayers

Give a copy of a recent newspaper to each row so that they can be shared out, one page to a few people. Invite the congregation to tear out the photographs or headlines which prompt them to think of things the church should be praying about. While adult-level songs are being sung, children should go to an area in which, under supervision, they can paste these cuttings on to large pieces of card. Invite three or four individuals or a family to stay at the front and lead prayers on some of the topics. (Remember to give instructions as to what is to be done with the left-over paper!)

Flame of praise

Give everyone a postcard-sized piece of paper, either red or orange or yellow. Talk about fire as a symbol of the Holy Spirit and ask members of the congregation to write on the paper a sentence of praise that they want the Holy Spirit to communicate to God the Father (if they are too young to write, they should draw on it some things they want to thank God for, if they are too young to draw, they should do some doodles and squiggles for God – he will understand that they are meant as praise, Romans 8:26 tells us that is the Spirit's work). Ask the children to help you collect the papers and attach them with *Blu-tack* to a large white board in the flame-shaped pattern shown in the diagram. While this is being done, the adult congregation should sing the much-loved hymns about the Holy Spirit which are beyond the children's understanding. Read or describe some and encourage a closer look after the service.

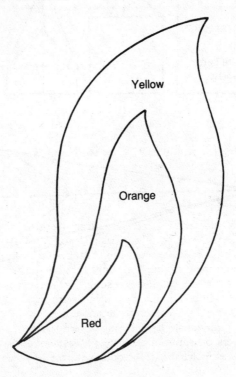

Flight of praise

Give everyone a sheet of rectangular paper bearing the words: 'The Lord God is . . .' Invite them to complete the sentence with a word or phrase of praise (adults helping non-writers). Then show the congregation how to fold their paper into a paper dart. At a given moment, everyone may launch their dart across the room. If one lands near them, they should read the words of praise on it, then relaunch it for someone else to share. The leader should have a clear pre-arranged signal for this chaotic act of praise to end.

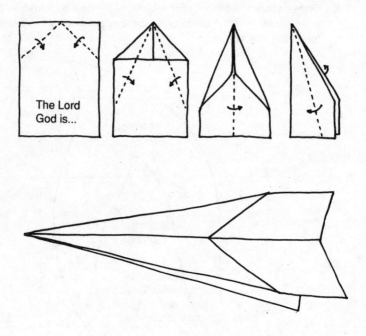

Thanking God for our possessions

Give everyone a sheet of A5 paper. Ask them to fold it in half in the middle of the longer side, then to tear from it a rectangular shape from the corner, and a square shape from the fold (it is easier to demonstrate this than to describe it – the shaded parts of the diagram are the ones to remove). When they open the paper, they will discover the shape of a suitcase. Ask the congregation to imagine that they are fleeing from their homes – not because they want a holiday, but because of an emergency. They cannot carry much in their suitcase, but they can take three favourite possessions. What would they take? Invite them to draw or write their chosen possessions on the paper, and to show those around them what they have drawn. The leader should then say a prayer thanking God for these favourite items, including a silence in which people may focus on their own choices. As a corporate thanksgiving, the suitcases could be collected by stewards for the leader to place on a table with the words of 1 Chronicles 29:11–13.

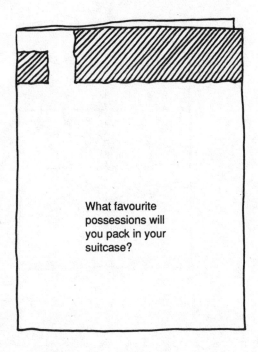

What favourite
possessions will
you pack in your
suitcase?

Taking people to the cross

Ask everyone to take a piece of A5 or A6 paper from under or near their seats. Demonstrating as you go along, get everyone to fold the paper in half vertically and then about a third of the way down horizontally. When opened up it looks like a cross. Ask them to write or draw in each of the four parts a person or situation they want to bring to Jesus in prayer. They could be people who are ill, people who do not realise how much Jesus loves them, friends who are far away or simply people they love. Ask adults to help the children near them. Ask stewards to collect the papers and take them to the front of the room. Lift them up while a silence is kept. Then use this response:

Leader: Jesus, we bring these people to your cross.
All: In your mercy, help them Lord. Amen.

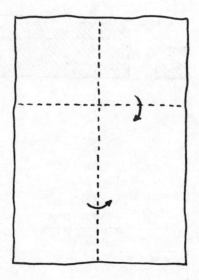

Prayers for healing

Display on the walls of the room huge hands cut from A1 sized card, one hand for every forty members of the congregation. Invite them to form groups of four or five and give each group a piece of A5 sized coloured paper and a felt pen. One member of the group should draw round his or her hand on the paper. The group should, between them, think of people they know who are sick and write their names inside the outline. There might also be groups for whom they wish to pray, such as deaf people or those who are HIV positive. One person from each group should attach the paper to the cut-outs of hands with *Blu-tack*. The leader should pray for the healing of all those who have been named, and, under the hands, display the caption, 'Jesus stretched out his hand and touched them . . . Be healed . . . Luke 5:13'. This could be made into a more lasting display on which names are added and subtracted as weeks go by.

Worship using simple movement

Hands praising God

The congregation performs appropriate hand actions as they respond to the leader:

Leader: We lift our hands to you, Lord,
All: We lift our hands to you.
Leader: We want to worship you, Lord,
All: We want to worship you.
Leader: We open hands to you, Lord,
All: We open hands to you.
Leader: What you want we will do, Lord,
All: What you want we will do.
Leader: We join our hands for you, Lord,
All: We join our hands for you.
Leader: We serve each other too, Lord,
All: We serve each other too.
Leader: We clap in praise of you, Lord,
All: We clap in praise of you.

Using Romans 5:8–11

Read the passage, then allow the congregation to copy a small group who are demonstrating the actions as the words are read again:

God has shown us how much he loves us, (*clasp hands on heart*).
We were God's enemies, (*clench fists aggressively*),
but he made us his friends, (*cross arms across chest*),
through the death of his Son, (*arms outstretched*).
Now that we are God's friends, (*cross arms across chest again*),
how much more will we be saved by Christ's life, (*raise open hands from hip level to chest level*).
But that is not all; we rejoice because of what God has done, (*hands high in praise*),
through our Lord Jesus Christ, who has now made us God's friends, (*cross arms across chest*).

Involving five senses

Give everyone a short stick of celery. Invite them to look at its curious shape as you thank God for the gift of sight, then to feel it as you thank God for the sense of touch. Go on to smell it, listen to it crunch as everyone breaks it in half at the same time, and finally taste it, thanking God for each sense in turn. The same could be done with a little water in a disposable cup.

Giving thanks

Give each member (or group) of the congregation a deflated balloon. On it they are to write in felt pen one thing that has happened recently for which they wish to thank God. They should then blow up the balloons and, all together, let them go. They may pick up and read any that land near them, so as to share the thanksgiving of others. They might even blow them up again and keep the words of thanks circulating.

Using 2 Chronicles 6:18–21

One person should perform the actions in italics, while another reads the passage:

Can you, O God, really live on earth among men and women? (*raise hand to indicate God, then sweep it to indicate men and women*).

Not even all heaven is large enough to hold you (*circle arms wide*),

so how can this Temple that I have built be large enough? (*Cup hands as if holding something tiny*).

Lord, my God, I am your servant (*stand straight, looking upward*).

Listen to my prayer and grant the requests I make to you (*touch mouth, then lift hands*).

Watch over this Temple day and night (*repeat cupping of hands, then hold them to heart*).

You have promised that this is where you will be worshipped, so hear me when I face this Temple and pray (*turn away from congregation*).

Hear my prayers and the prayers of your people when they face this place and pray (*rotate, sweeping arm as if gathering all the congregation in, and face away from them again*).

In your home in heaven, hear us and forgive us (*slowly sink to knees*).

Dance of God's presence

Use actions seriously and symbolically to 'God be in my head', the music of which is in most older hymn books:

God be in my head (*touch head*),
And in my understanding (*lift hands upward*).
God be in my eyes (*touch eyes*),
And in my looking (*point hand outward*).
God be in my mouth (*touch mouth*),
And in my speaking (*drop hands downward*).
God be in my heart (*touch chest*),
And in my thinking (*cross arms across chest*).
God be at my end (*hands by side*),
And at my departing (*bow head*).

Dance of adoration

Invite the congregation to cluster into small groups, adults and children together. Remind them of this simple song of praise, the music for which can be found in *Mission Praise, Songs of Fellowship*, and many other recent hymn books:

Father we adore you,
Lay our lives before you,
How we love you.

In their groups they are to devise an appropriate movement or action to go with each line. After several minutes, sing the song with its verses about Jesus and the Spirit as well, with everyone simultaneously performing the different actions they devised.

Fruit of the spirit

Pass a bunch of seedless grapes around the congregation and invite everyone to take one. Read Galatians 5:22–23 and talk briefly about the ways of pleasing God that the Holy Spirit wants to release in every Christian. Read it again, asking everyone to select one which they know could feature more strongly in the way they live. Then say this prayer with a short pause between each quality of fruit and suggest that, to make the prayer personal, the congregation should listen for the one they chose and eat their grape at that moment:

'Father God, only with the help of the Holy Spirit can we truly please you. Fill us with the Spirit so that our lives may overflow with love, joy, peace, patience, kindness, goodness, faithfulness, humility, self-control. May we who have tasted your goodness live lives that show your goodness to others. Amen.'

Wave of praise

Teach the congregation the 'Mexican wave'. Those sitting on the extreme left of the room stand, lift their arms into the air, lower their arms and sit. A fraction later, those sitting on their right copy the motion, and so on, so that a wave seems to pass through the crowd. Use this as an action of praise to God. Read Psalm 93. Whenever the word 'sea' (or 'ocean' in the Good News Bible) is mentioned, the congregation repeats the wave of praise.

Using Psalm 99:1–5

Read the psalm, encouraging the congregation to accompany it with hand actions. They should be demonstrated by a group first, then copied by everyone, remaining seated, as the psalm is read:

Verse 1a: Both hands pointed upward, high above head.
1b: Hands trembling.
2: Sweep hands in wide arc to sides.
3: Cup hands together and raise them.
4: Clench fists.
5: Put hands together in prayerful attitude and kneel or bow heads. Hold this position in silence for a few seconds.

Forgiveness for prejudice

Ask a few people of differing ages to join you at the front of the room and be blindfolded. Feed them three different items, all of which have been dyed blue with food colouring (e.g. mashed potato, milk, rice pudding, marzipan). Ask them to guess what the foods have in common and, when they fail to guess, take off their blindfolds and enjoy their reactions! Mention the judgments we make about people without even getting to know their true character, because of their skin colour or other differences. Lead into a prayer asking for forgiveness for judging people solely by their appearance.

Struck dumb

Invite everyone to imagine that, like Zechariah, they were not able to speak for a while. A priest's job was to lead the worship of God's people, and to worship is our task, too. So if words were not available to you, what would you do with your body in order to show God the love and praise you have for him? Optionally, you could invite the congregation to talk to those next to them about the possibilities. Then ask for silence, and invite everyone to perform the action which they have thought of in praise of God. While they hold the gesture there should be a few seconds of silence, then words from Zechariah's prophecy should be read (Luke 1:68–69, 78–79).

Using Psalm 133

Read Psalm 133:1, then invite the congregation to talk together in groups about how, by arranging and shaping their own bodies, they can form a human sculpture which symbolises that verse. After a couple of minutes, invite them to adopt the position they thought of. While they are in position, read the whole of the psalm.

Using Isaiah 55:6–11

As the passage is read, three people should perform appropriate movements. They begin in a straight line with backs to the congregation:

Turn to the Lord (*face front*),
and pray to him now that he is near (*hands in an attitude of prayer*).
Let the wicked leave their way of life (*twist awkwardly away from the front*),
and change their way of thinking (*still twisted, sink to knees*).
Let them turn to the Lord our God (*turn to front and lift heads*).
He is merciful and quick to forgive (*stand*).
'My thoughts', says the Lord (*hands high*),
'Are not like yours (*touch fingers to head*),
And my ways are different from yours (*repeat last two actions*).
As high as the heavens are above the earth, so high are my ways and thoughts above yours (*left actor stretches as high as possible, right actor grovels as low as possible, middle actor bridges the two*).
My word is like the snow and the rain that comes down from the sky to water the earth (*pattering fingers start high and sink to floor*).
They make the crops grow and provide seed for sowing and food to eat (*fingers creeping upward from floor and waving up to a great height*).
So also will be the word that I speak (*return to position for 'As high as'*).
It will not fail to do what I plan for it; it will do everything I send it to do ('*high' actor raises middle actor to feet, middle actor raises 'low' actor to feet; finish in position for 'And pray to him'*).

Using Hosea 14:1–9

Ask a reader and a group of between four and ten adults to prepare this visual interpretation of Hosea 14:1–9:

Verse 1: The movers, who are scattered across a space, run together. As they group in the centre they sink to one knee on 'fall'.

2: Scoop hands together and lift them as if offering a precious gift, rising again.

3: Walk apart, shaking heads.

4: Repeat the first movement, running together into a group.

5–6: All push their hands into the centre of the cluster at waist level, then slowly raise them above their heads (like a single shoot growing) and as they reach their height spread their arms out in a random pattern, fingers stretched (like branches growing out of a trunk).

7–8a: The pair at the front of the cluster form an arch, through which all the others pass, spreading out in different directions across the space.

8b: On 'I am', repeat the first movement, running together into a group.

9: They lead off in a very sedate line. The last person in the line turns to look back, stumbles, then regains balance and rejoins the straight line. Exit.

Reconciliation

Ask two people to present a (rehearsed) mime of having a fearful argument. This should last about twenty seconds and contain no sound at all. Ask the congregation to cluster into groups of two or three and identify the gestures which show that the people had no peace. After some time, ask the pair to mime a reconciliation, again using gestures only. The adults and children of the congregation should again identify how movements revealed emotions. Follow this with a corporate symbol of the peace which God intends should unite the congregation. This could be a pause in the service during which everyone can address those around them, giving one of the gestures of reconciliation and using the response below. Ensure that the actions take place across the generations and between strangers, not just among friends.

A: God's peace be with you.
B: And with you too.

Action creed

Teach and then use this statement, with its appropriate actions, after each phrase:

Jesus died, (*stretch arms wide*),
Jesus was buried, (*head bowed, arms wrapped around body*),
Jesus rose from the dead (*palms open, arms raised above head*).

Leader: We believe God sent his Son to live in our world . . .
We believe that he died instead of us and provides a way for us to know God . . .
We believe that many people saw Jesus risen from the dead; that he defeated death once and for all . . .
We believe that Jesus returned to heaven and rules now with God the Father . . .
We look forward to the day when Jesus will return and take us to be with him forever . . .

Hot and cold behaviour

Invite the congregation to close their eyes, hold their hands in front of their faces and blow on them. Feel the cold air. 'Sometimes our words or attitudes toward people are cold or unfriendly, we make them shiver or give them the cold shoulder. Forgive us, Lord, for this.' Tell them to breathe heat onto their hands. Feel the hot air. 'Sometimes our attitude to people is too heated, we get angry and go red. Forgive us, Lord, for this.' Tell people to smile warmly. 'It feels good to smile, warm and friendly. Other people feel comfortable with us and the things we say are pleasant. Encourage us, Lord, to be like this. Amen.'

Evening prayer

Lighten our darkness (*hands in front of eyes*),
Lord we pray (*remove hands from eyes*),
and in your mercy defend us (*hands in 'praying' position*),
from all perils and dangers of this night (*cross arms across chest*),
for the love of your only Son (*hold hands open in front of chest*), our Saviour, Jesus Christ (*hands in air*). Amen.

© *The Alternative Service Book*, 1980.

Thanking God for forgiveness

Line by line, the congregation repeats the words and movements after the leader:

Sin hurts, (*hit self with clenched hands*),
Sin hurts God, (*point upwards*),
Sin hurts others, (*point forwards*),
Sin hurts me, (*point to self*).
Jesus has forgiven us, (*right hand up, palm forward*),
And set us free, (*left hand up as well*),
Thank you God, (*both hands lifted high*).

God's care for every part of me

Invite the congregation to feel (or pull out!) a hair. Recalling God's individual care, read Luke 21:18, then use this response:

Leader: God cares for me.
All: God cares for every part of me.

Go on to lead the congregation to look at their hands as Isaiah 49:16 is read, and to cradle their arms as Psalm 131:2 is read, followed each time by the response.

Change of clothes

While one person reads these words, based on Colossians 3:8–12, a group or the whole congregation performs the actions:

God wants you to strip off the old self (*mime removing a jumper*). Strip off anger (*stamp foot*), hate (*shake fists*), rudeness (*tongue out*), lies (*finger to lips, 'Shh!'*). God wants you to put on the new self (*put on jumper*), clothe yourselves with kindness (*give money from pocket*), gentleness (*hug self*), patience (*fold arms*), love (*blow kiss*). You are the people of God; strip off the old self; clothe yourselves in the new.

Worship using silence

Leave your worries with him

Invite the congregation to sit with their eyes closed and their arms crossed. They are to think about the things which worry them and cling tight to them. Then they imagine Jesus to be sitting somewhere in the room facing them. Concentrate on him so that his compassionate smile is very clear. They stand, in their imaginations, and take their worries to Jesus. They put them, one at a time, in his lap and leave them there, returning to their seats without them. After a silence, the leader should read Matthew 11:28, 1 Peter 5:7 and Philippians 4:6–7.

Making room for Jesus

Ask children and adults to shut their eyes and imagine: 'You are in a queue, maybe for the school tuck shop, maybe for a bus or tube. Everyone is pushing and shoving to get to the front, but you push hardest and get there first. Then everything goes quiet and, looking round, you realise that the very last person in the queue is Jesus. How do you feel? Slowly and humbly, imagine that you invite Jesus to change places with you.'

Keep this exercise short so that children can concentrate on it. Follow it with prayers that we will never treat anyone badly because we think ourselves too important.

Praying hands

Invite everyone to spread out the fingers of one hand so that the thumb points to the chest. Suggest that they silently pray for four different people, touching their four fingers in turn. Finally they should touch the thumb and pray for themselves.

Praying for the locality

Split the congregation into various groups (the size does not matter). Allocate to each group one of the roads that surrounds the church and ask them, in a time of silence, to imagine themselves walking down that road, looking at the people and buildings they pass. As they travel in mind, they are to pray that the church may have an impact on the places they pass.

Meditating on Gethsemane

Invite the congregation to shut their eyes and imagine that they are Peter. They are to see themselves in the garden (a rocky garden on the side of a hill, with tough grass and short, fat trees) and, as you read it, take part in the story in their minds. When Peter moves in the story, they are to imagine themselves moving. When Jesus speaks, they imagine he is speaking to them. Read Matthew 26:36–46 quite slowly, with a pause between each sentence. After the meditation, ask some to tell you how Jesus looked in their mind's eye. Tired? Distressed? Defiant? Other Bible passages could be used on different occasions, such as John 13:2–15, Matthew 17:1–9 or John 21:3–13.

Thank you, sorry, please

Give everyone a teaspoon, and remind them of the abbreviation for it, TSP. This is also an abbreviation for one of the ways we can pray to God, saying to him, 'Thank you, Sorry, and Please'. The leader should say a three part prayer, with pauses in it during which the congregation can bring to God their own words of thanks, confession and request.

Confession

With short silences and closed eyes, talk the congregation through a three-part confession. Firstly fists should be clenched to help bring to mind wrong things we hold on tightly to. Then turn fists downwards and open hands as a sign of letting go the things we are sorry for and repent of. Finally, turn hands upward, with palms open, as a mark of receiving God's forgiveness.

9
FESTIVALS

Christmas

Seeing and adoring

Let us praise Jesus. Eternal King of Heaven, you were born
a tiny baby. In our minds and hearts . . .
Let us see you and adore you.
You have been endlessly worshipped by angels, but you
were glimpsed by humble shepherds. In our minds and
hearts . . .
Let us see you and adore you.
The whole world is yours for you created it, yet you were
laid in a cold, stone manger. In our minds and hearts . . .
Let us see you and adore you.
You are the glorious Lord of all, yet you came to earth
crying and helpless. In our minds and hearts . . .
Let us see you and adore you.
Accept the praises of those you came to serve and save.
Amen.

Thanksgiving

Having introduced a time of open sharing, news and prayer,
offer this segment of the service in the first instance to
children so that they can tell the congregation what they got
for Christmas. Subsequently open this to adults as well. Point
out that, just as Mary and Joseph took their most precious
Christmas present, Jesus himself, to dedicate him to God, we
can dedicate our presents to God to be used unselfishly and
wisely to please him. Either do this in a prayer or invite
several people to make a response.

Words of praise

Leader: Lord Jesus, gold is precious,
All: But to us, you are more precious.
Leader: Lord Jesus, frankincense smells lovely,
All: But to us, you are more lovely.
Leader: Lord Jesus, myrrh has a special and serious purpose,
All: But to us, you are more special.
Leader: We have no gold to give you,
All: So we give you our money.
Leader: We have no frankincense to give you,
All: So we give you our praise.
Leader: We have no myrrh to give you,
All: So we give you our lives. Amen.

For those who find Christmas hard

We pray for those who are lonely this Christmas because
they have few friends. Give them your peace, Lord,
And show us how to help them.
We pray for those who are sad because they are trying to
cope without someone they love. Give them your peace,
Lord,
And show us how to help them.
We pray for those who find several days shut in with their
families a real strain. Give them your peace, Lord,
And show us how to help them.
We pray for those who have felt obliged to spend too much
and face a worrying future. Give them your peace, Lord,
And show us how to help them.
We pray for those who have not heard that you were born
on earth as a human being, and don't realise why there
is such good news to celebrate. Give them your peace,
Lord,
And show us how to help them.

Thanksgiving game

Invite the congregation to form groups with a pencil and some paper. Ask one person from each group to come to the front of the room – neither the youngest nor the oldest, someone in the middle. Whisper to them an object connected with the Christmas story. They must return to the group and draw it. The person who guesses what it is returns to the front and, when he or she has given the answer, is told the next object to draw, and so on. The first drawing is of a sheep; subsequently tell the representatives to draw a star, a manger, an angel, a shepherd, strips of cloth (swaddling clothes), three wise men. If there is a congregation of several hundred, four or five leaders will be needed to whisper the objects. When about two thirds of the groups have finished, stop the game and congratulate everyone for taking part. Invite each group to thank God for Christmas. Any member of the group who wishes to can choose one of the things that have been drawn and say, 'Thank you, God, for . . .' Point out that it is quite acceptable for individuals to give their thanks to God silently if they prefer.

Mothering Sunday

Creative prayers

Give everyone a sheet of size A4 paper. Demonstrate three ways of tearing the paper, inviting the congregation to copy you. Fold the paper in half and tear from it a traditional house shape. Talk about living together and lead a prayer asking God to increase the joy found by those who live in homes where adults and children are together. Then refold the paper and tear from it a heart. Ask the congregation to focus on it as you thank God for those who give love and care, especially mothers. Fold the paper again and tear a pair of ears. Focussing on listening to each other, ask God to forgive the times when communication breaks down and people hurt those with whom they live. Choose words which are sensitive to those for whom motherhood suggests pain rather than warmth. See the illustration overleaf.

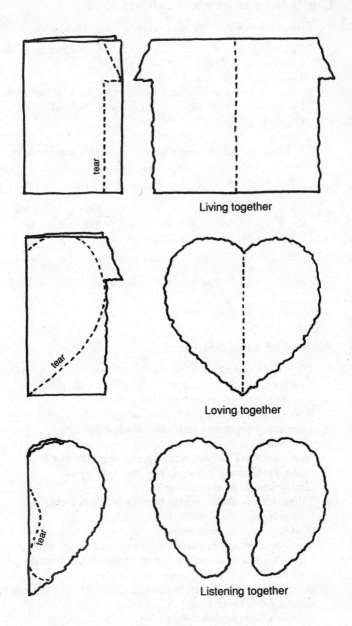

Living together

Loving together

Listening together

God's love is like a mother's love

Using Isaiah 66:13; 49:15, Psalm 131:2 and Matthew 23:37.

Isaiah wrote that God is a mother to us, comforting us and carrying us in her arms. Glorious God . . .
Thank you for your loving care.

He also wrote that God would never forget any one of us. He knows us each like a mother knows her children. Glorious God . . .
Thank you for your loving care.

David wrote that in God's presence he was quiet and at peace, trusting God like a child safe in his mother's loving arms. Glorious God . . .
Thank you for your loving care.

Jesus spoke of himself as a mother, longing to wrap his arms around his people like a mother hen gathers her chicks under her wings. Glorious God . . .
Thank you for your loving care.

For all those you have given us to care for us, and for the assurance that your love for us is endless, glorious God . . .
Thank you for your loving care.

Prayer of confession

Holy God, parent of us all, we know we don't always treat each other as you want us to. Lord God, forgive us,
And help us to be more loving.

There are times when we insist on getting our own way despite what others feel. Lord God, forgive us,
And help us to be more loving.

Sometimes we increase the tension when we ought to be seeking to make peace. Lord God, forgive us,
And help us to be more loving.

Often we say things which hurt each other. Lord God, forgive us,
And help us to be more loving.

For our jealousy, our lack of respect, and times when we won't listen to those we live with, Lord God, forgive us,
And help us to be more loving.

And because we sometimes just get bored with each other, Lord God, forgive us,
And help us to be more loving.

Prayer of thanksgiving

Give everyone present a piece of paper and a pencil. They are to tear and fold it into the shape of a traditional house, as illustrated. Inside it they are to draw pin-people to represent everyone who lives at home with them. They may also draw their pets and anyone who visits their home so regularly that they are effectively part of their 'family' (so, for example, single people who live alone should not necessarily just draw themselves). In the roof they are to write, 'Thank you, Lord God' (make sure that adults help children with this). Then stewards should collect all the drawings and carry them on trays to the front of the room. The leader of the service says a prayer of thanksgiving for everyone who has been drawn, and all the 'houses' should be placed reverently on the table.

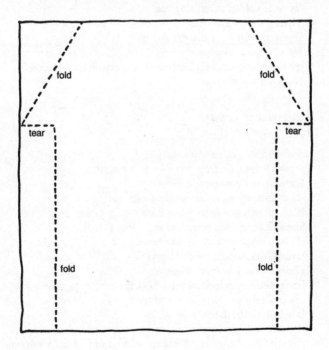

Palm Sunday

Based on Zechariah 9:9–12

Rejoice, rejoice, people of Jersualem.
Shout for joy all people.
Look, your king is coming to you.
Shout for joy all people.
He comes triumphant and victorious.
Shout for joy all people.
He comes humble and riding on a donkey.
Shout for joy all people.
Your king will make peace among the nations.
Shout for joy all people.
He will rule from sea to sea.
Shout for joy all people.
The Lord will set his people free.
Shout for joy all people.
He will come with blessing to all who have suffered.
Shout for joy all people.

Welcoming Jesus

Jesus Christ, ride into our universe.
We welcome you here as our king.
Jesus Christ, ride on to our planet earth.
We welcome you here as our king.
Jesus Christ, ride throughout our nation.
We welcome you here as our king.
Jesus Christ, ride into (*name of your town*).
We welcome you here as our king.
Jesus Christ, ride up this street.
We welcome you here as our king.
Jesus Christ, ride into this church.
We welcome you here as our king.
Jesus Christ, ride into my life.
We welcome you here as our king.
King of the universe, King of our nation, King of (*your town*), King of this church, my king.
We welcome you here as our king.

Acclamation

Leader: Blessed is he who comes in the name of the Lord.
All: Hosanna in the highest! Hosanna in the highest!
Leader: Peace in heaven and glory in the highest.
All: God will save us! God will save us!

Leaves of praise

Give everyone a piece of green paper and invite them to fold it lengthways and tear from it an arc shape, so that when it is opened it resembles a palm leaf. On it they should write a word which describes Jesus (e.g. great, gentle, king, humble). Those who are too young to write may draw a picture of Jesus, and those too young to draw may make some squiggles on the paper in praise of him. When this is finished, sing an appropriate song while everyone waves their leaves in praise of Christ. This could be developed in different ways – throwing the leaves down in a particular way as on the Jerusalem road, or attaching them to a paper tree trunk which has already been fitted to a wall. Encourage the congregation to read what everyone else wrote.

Greeting the King

Learn this response, based on Matthew 21:5.

Leader: Tell the city of Jersualem:
All: Look, your king is coming to you.

Repeat it many times, inserting the names of towns and villages in the locality of the church, e.g., 'Tell the city of Birmingham. . . , tell the town of Kings Heath. . . , tell the village of Lickey. . .'.

Good Friday

Thanks and praise

For your death on the cross, which you could have escaped
but chose not to, Lord Jesus . . .
We remember with thanks and praise.
For the pain of the cross, which you endured because you
loved us, Lord Jesus . . .
We remember with thanks and praise.
For the sacrifice of the cross, which meant you could take
the punishment we deserve instead of us, Lord Jesus . . .
We remember with thanks and praise.
For the victory of the cross, which could not defeat you,
for you were raised to life again forever, Lord Jesus . . .
We remember with thanks and praise.
For the symbol of the cross, which allows us never to forget
the great love you have poured out on us, Lord Jesus . . .
We remember with thanks and praise.
For the power of the cross, which has won us forgiveness
and reconciled us to God, Lord Jesus . . .
We remember with thanks and praise.

Intercessions

Jesus died because of the weakness of those in government.
We pray for those in government today, especially . . .
Jesus died because of the scheming of religious leaders.
We pray for those who lead the church today, especially . . .
Jesus was humiliated at his trial and deserted by his friends.
We pray for all who suffer as social outcasts today, especially
. . .
Jesus hung on a cross and suffered unimaginable pain. We
pray for all who are in pain today, especially . . .
Jesus' family and friends had to face life without him. We
pray for all those who suffer loss today, especially . . .
May the God who knows what it is like to be human help
all who are in need. Amen.

Assurance of forgiveness

The good thing about the crucifixion, the 'Good' in 'Good Friday', is that when Jesus died it was as if he was taking the blame for our sins instead of us. Suggest that everyone assures each other of God's forgiveness by going around drawing a cross with one finger on the palms of other members of the congregation and saying, God has forgiven us.'

Forgiven through the cross

Give everyone a sheet of A4 paper, and show them how to fold and tear it in the manner illustrated so as to make a cross. The leader should say a prayer of confession. Then encourage the congregation to exchange their crosses with someone else, with the words: 'Because of the cross, we are forgiven.'

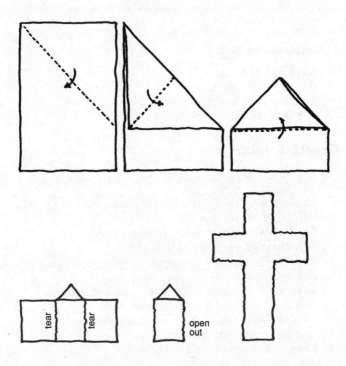

Confession

Leader: Lord, forgive the sleep of the disciples,
All: And forgive me when I am too tired to pray.
Leader: Forgive the rage of the crowd,
All: And forgive me when I can't control my anger.
Leader: Forgive the deceit of Judas,
All: And forgive me when I let Jesus down.
Leader: Forgive the violence of the man with the sword,
All: And forgive me when my temper gets the better of me.
Leader: Forgive the cowardice of those who deserted Jesus,
All: And forgive me when I lose the chance to witness for him.
Leader: Lord, we need the forgiveness you died to bring,
All: Have mercy on us, Lord. Amen.

Easter

Using Romans 6:9

Leader: I know,
All: And we know,
Leader: That Christ has been raised from death,
All: And he'll never die again.

Greeting Jesus

Leader: Lord Jesus we greet you.
All: Risen from the dead.
Leader: We thought your love had reached a dead end.
All: Now we see it is the way to life.
Leader: We thought your life was wasted.
All: Now we see it is raised in glory.
Leader: We thought your suffering was pointless.
All: Now we see God's purpose in it all.
Leader: We thought death was the end of you.
All: Now we see life triumph over death.
Leader: We thought this life was pointless.
All: Now you have given us hope.
Leader: Lord Jesus we greet you.
All: Risen from the dead.

In praise of Jesus

People say that God is dead,
Let us praise the risen Lord,
We know we can shout instead,
Let us praise the risen Lord,
Peter looked inside the tomb,
Let us praise the risen Lord,
Left confused and full of gloom,
Let us praise the risen Lord,
Jesus came to him to say,
Let us praise the risen Lord,
'I'm alive. It's Easter Day!'
Let us praise the risen Lord,
'God is dead' just isn't true,
Let us praise the risen Lord,
I believe that! How about you?
Let us praise the risen Lord.

Thanksgiving for Jesus' death and resurrection

Lord Jesus, I'm sad that wicked men treated you so cruelly. You
went through it for my sake.
Thank you, Lord Jesus.
I'm sad that you were whipped and insulted. You went through
it for my sake.
Thank you, Lord Jesus.
I'm sad that soldiers spat at you and dressed you in stupid
clothes. You went through it for my sake.
Thank you, Lord Jesus.
I'm sad that you were nailed to a cross and died there gasping
for breath. You went through it for my sake.
Thank you, Lord Jesus.
I'm sad that you didn't even have your own grave, but were
laid in a borrowed one. You went through it for my sake.
Thank you, Lord Jesus.
But I'm glad, very glad, wonderfully glad, that three days later
you came alive again and will never die. You went through
it for my sake.
Thank you, Lord Jesus.

Symbols of hope

Give everyone a tiny chocolate egg wrapped in foil. Invite them to eat the chocolate, then to take the foil and model it into a shape which will be, for them, a symbol of hope to take away from the service. It might be an empty cross, an anchor, a living man or anything else that their mind strtetches to. Ask adults to help very young children to think of ideas, or to mould it into a pretty, abstract shape as an act of worship to God. After a few minutes ask them to show to those around them what they have created. Optionally, ask some to call out what they have made and why it will help them remember the living Jesus.

Dedication to Christ

Holy One of God, to the Jewish leaders you were a threat,
But in my heart you will be king.
To Pilate you were a nuisance,
But in my heart you will be king.
To the soldiers you were an object of mockery,
But in my heart you will be king.
To the women you were much to be pitied,
But in my heart you will be king.
To the rulers you were a figure to scorn,
But in my heart you will be king.

Using 1 Corinthians 15:51–58

Leader: Listen, I tell you a mystery!
All: We shall not die, but we shall all be changed.
Leader: Death has been swallowed up in victory.
All: Where, O death, is your victory?
Leader: The sting of death is sin.
All: Where, O death, is your sting?
Leader: God gives us the victory through our Lord Jesus Christ.
All: Thanks be to God!
Leader: Therefore, stand firm.
All: Nothing will move us.
Leader: Always give yourselves fully to the work of the Lord.
All: We know that our work for the Lord is not in vain.

Glory to Jesus

Glory to you for rising from the dead. Risen Lord Jesus . . .
My Lord and my God.
Glory to you for your victorious triumph. Risen Lord Jesus . . .
My Lord and my God.
Glory to you that death has lost its sting. Risen Lord Jesus . . .
My Lord and my God.
Glory to you that eternal life is won for us all. Risen Lord
  Jesus . . .
My Lord and my God.
Glory to you that doubt can give way to belief. Risen Lord
  Jesus . . .
My Lord and my God.
Glory to you that fear can give way to praise. Risen Lord
  Jesus . . .
My Lord and my God.

Ending

Arrange in advance for a young girl to lead a procession.
Give her a basket of spices or other sweet-smelling materials.
She should lead the entire congregation out of the room.
Explain that they are to walk all the way round the church
building as if they are searching for Jesus' body. When they
get back to the door they went out of, it will be locked, so
they should wait there until everyone has gathered. Then the
girl should knock loudly on the door. The leader will open
it, so that this exchange can take place:

Leader: What are you looking for?
Girl: We are looking for Jesus Christ.
Leader: His body is not here.
Girl: Why is it not here?
Leader: Alleluia! Christ is risen!
All: He is risen indeed. Alleluia!

Finish the service there, outside the building, with a simple
and familiar song of praise. If the structure of the church
building or the weather make this impossible, the congregation should turn to face the main door of the room, which
should be closed. The girl should knock on it and the leader
open it from the outside. After the exchange described above
has taken place, sing a suitable closing hymn. (Don't forget
to make special arrangements for the disabled or elderly.)

Pentecost

Invocation

Leader: Spirit, be there at the start,
All: Spirit, remain in my heart.
Leader: Spirit, renewed every hour,
All: Spirit, fill me with your power.
Leader: Spirit, renewed every day,
All: Spirit, to show me God's way.
Leader: Spirit, be there at the end,
All: Spirit, be there as my friend.

Based on Romans 8:26

Holy Spirit, increase our understanding of God.
Spirit, also come to help us.
Holy Spirit, show us what God wants us to do.
Spirit, also come to help us.
Holy Spirit, remind us of the truth about Jesus.
Spirit, also come to help us.
Holy Spirit, tell God what we are praying about.
Spirit, also come to help us.
Holy Spirit, allow us to tell others the good news about
  Jesus.
Spirit, also come to help us. Amen.

Fill us with the Spirit

Leader: Where the Spirit of the Lord is,
All: There is love for one another.
Leader: Where the Spirit of the Lord is,
All: There is power to make our faith strong.
Leader: Where the Spirit of the Lord is,
All: There is light to help us understand God.
Leader: Where the Spirit of the Lord is,
All: There is freedom in God's family.
Leader: Where the Spirit of the Lord is,
All: There is certainty of our future in Heaven.
Leader: Fill us, Lord, with the rich blessing you promise
  your people,
All: Fill us, Lord, with your Holy Spirit.

Prayer

Leader: Where the Spirit of the Lord is,
All: There is love for one another.
Leader: Where the Spirit of the Lord is,
All: There is power to make our faith strong.
Leader: Where the Spirit of the Lord is,
All: There is joy that's more than words can say.
Leader: Where the Spirit of the Lord is,
All: There is freedom in God's family.
Leader: Where the Spirit of the Lord is,
All: There is sharing of the good news.
Leader: Set us on fire in the service of God,
All: Fill us, Lord God, with your Spirit.

The active Holy Spirit

When Jesus lived his power was real,
We have a God who works today,
The Spirit gave him strength to heal,
We have a God who works today,
His followers could heal the lame,
We have a God who works today,
The Spirit used them just the same,
We have a God who works today,
His power has never gone away,
We have a God who works today,
The Spirit works in all who pray,
We have a God who works today,
We too must tread where Jesus trod,
We have a God who works today,
The Spirit is the power of God,
We have a God who works today.

Praise round the world

Ask those in the congregation who speak foreign languages
to say 'Praise to Jesus Christ the Lord', one after the other,
in their chosen language as in Acts 2:6. Follow this with a
time of open prayer in a variety of languages, praising God
as the Holy Spirit leads.

Come Holy Spirit

Leader: Spirit of the Holy God, fill this church.
All: Holy Spirit, come as a flame.
Leader: Set us on fire with love for you.
All: Holy Spirit come as a wind.
Leader: Sweep through us with your unseen power.
All: Holy Spirit, come as water.
Leader: Wash away all that spoils our lives.
All: Holy Spirit, come as oil.
Leader: Anoint us to work in your service.
All: Holy Spirit come as breath.
Leader: Make us alive with enthusiasm for you.
All: Holy Spirit, come as a dove.
Leader: Bring us together in peace with one another.
All: Spirit of the Holy God, fill this church. Amen.

Open thanksgiving

Invite everyone in the congregation to find a partner. If they are under twenty, they must find someone over twenty and vice versa. (Obviously, some chuches will adjust the age to match the spread of their congregation; the exact make-up of the pairs is not important as long as it prompts a reasonable interaction of adults with children and teenagers. Young children should take a parent with them if they are going to partner a stranger.) In their pairs, they should answer the question: 'What are you most thankful for that the Holy Spirit has given you?' Make sure that adults listen to children, even if their answers appear slight, and that they speak to the children in a way that explains simply. Then split a time of sharing, praise and prayer into two parts. Firstly those under twenty are given time to say thank you to God without older people interrupting their simplicity. Then open the time to adults as well. Stress that if any pairs mentioned spiritual gifts as they talked together, this would be an appropriate time to use them.

Remembrance Sunday

Why we remember

Preface the silence with this reading for two people, and end it with the verse by Algernon Swinburne.

A: Why should we remember?

B: How should we remember?

A: We should remember that some of the freedoms we enjoy most were bought at a cost. When the wars of our nations beckoned, millions of men and women saw no alternative but to fight so that those who were oppressed could be free.

B: So we should remember with gratitude.

A: We should remember that this century has lost the potential of milions of young lives; spent as the price of victory, wasted as the price of failure.

B: So we should remember with shame.

A: We should remember that the suffering, the sorrow and the dying are not just part of history, for in this century the 'war that would end all wars' has happened again and again and again and again.

B: So we should remember with determination to be peacemakers.

A: We should remember that ours is a God who loves peace and longs for the time, which will surely come, when the swords of war will be hammered into the ploughshares which bring food to the hungry.

B: So we should remember with hope.

A: Let us remember prayerfully.

B: With two minutes of silence, let us remember. (*Silence*).

B: And time remembered is grief forgotten,
And frosts are slain and flowers begotten,
And in green underwood and cover,
Blossom by blossom the Spring begins.

Remembering and praying

Leader: Father God, at this time of remembrance, we weep
for the waste that war brings, we pray for those who still
bear the scars, and we remember with thanks those who
have given their lives so that we might live in freedom.
(*Silence.*) Make faith prevail over fear, make justice prevail
over force, make truth prevail over lies, and make love
and peace prevail over all things. Amen.

Advent

Ready to serve Jesus

Invite the congregation to cluster into groups of three or
four, adults and children together. Ask them to make a mental
list of things that Jesus would be disappointed to see us doing
when he returns (remind adults not to make their contributions childish). After a minute, invite some to suggest what
they decided. The leader should then say a prayer asking for
forgiveness, mentioning these by name. Then ask the groups
to consider what Jesus would be pleased to see us doing when
he comes back. After hearing suggestions as before, the leader
should pray that we will be more willing to serve in these
ways.

Looking forward

Leader: Lord Jesus, as we look forward to celebrating your
first coming at Christmas,
All: May we be prepared for your second coming.
Leader: Come, Lord, with triumph,
All: But may we not be ashamed.
Leader: Come, Lord, with glory,
All: But may we not be caught unprepared.
Leader: Come, Lord, as a judge,
All: But may we be forgiven.
Leader: Come, Lord, as our king,
All: And may we rejoice as never before.
Leader: It will be the greatest of all days,
All: We will live with you forever. Alleluia! Praise the Lord!

Based on Isaiah 40:1–9

Leader: God says, 'Comfort my people. Comfort them!'

All: We have all suffered long enough. Our sins are now forgiven.

Leader: Prepare in the wilderness a road for the Lord. Clear a way in the desert for our God.

All: The glory of the Lord is about to be revealed. All mankind will see it.

Leader: Proclaim a message!

All: What message shall we proclaim?

Leader: Proclaim that all mankind are like grass; they last no longer than wild flowers. Grass withers and flowers fade,

All: But the word of our God endures forever.

Leader: Go up on a high mountain and call out with a loud voice,

All: Good news! Good news!

Leader: Speak out and do not be afraid,

All: Our God is coming!

Ready rap

Everyone clicks their fingers on the stressed syllables.

Jesus is coming,
Let's get ready,
Maybe this year,
Let's get ready,
Maybe ten years,
Let's get ready,
Maybe thousands,
Let's get ready.
Are you preparing?
Let's get ready,
Gonna be a party,
Let's get ready,
You're invited,
Let's get ready,
Will you be ready?
Let's get ready,
Don't disappoint him,
Let's get ready,
Let's get ready,
Let's get ready, Yeah!

Bible Sunday

Rhyme for young children

Teach the words and actions, then say them together:

Jesus, I am loved by you, (*hands crossed over chest*),
The Bible tells me this is true, (*hands opened side by side, as
  if reading a book*).
Help me turn away from wrong, (*turn from left to right*),
Let me please you all day long, (*hands in the air*).

Prayers of confession

Pray that, as a nation, we may rediscover what the Bible says
about God, about ethics, about justice, about community. As
a prayer of confession, a teenage boy should read Psalm
119:9–16. After each verse, he says, 'For the times when we
have failed to do this. . .'. All reply, 'Forgive us, merciful
God.'

Intercessions

Lord God, we pray for all those who use the Bible to teach
  and preach. Help them to be thorough, but not boring.
  Long ago you gave us the Bible,
May it challenge and change us today.
For scholars who study the Bible in the light of twentieth
  century knowledge. Help them to be open-minded, but
  not unbelieving. Long ago you gave us the Bible,
May it challenge and change us today.
For those who translate the Bible into new languages. Help
  them to be accurate, but always relevant. Long ago you
  gave us the Bible,
May it challenge and change us today.
For all who hear the Christmas readings this month. May
  they sound comforting and familiar, yet be full of new
  insights. Long ago you gave us the Bible,
May it challenge and change us today.

10
ORDERS OF SERVICE

Structured all-age service

Welcome.

Leader: In God's presence we have gathered together as his family, and we have come to give him praise.
All: Help us, Lord, to praise you.
Leader: To hear what he wants to teach us through the Bible.
All: Help us, Lord, to learn from you.
Leader: To pray to him about the needs of the world.
All: Help us, Lord, to pray to you.
Leader: To ask him to forgive our sins.
All: Help us, Lord, to be truly sorry.
Leader: And to enjoy the friendship of our brothers and sisters in Christ.
All: Help us, Lord, to love each other.
Leader: Let us shout for joy to the Lord who loves us.
All: Great is the Lord and most worthy of praise.

Hymn of praise.

Leader: Now is the time to turn to God and seek his mercy, for we have strayed from his ways like lost sheep, but like a good shepherd he has sought us and saved us, and longs to forgive our sins.

Leader: For the actions which have angered you, we are truly sorry,

All: In your mercy, Lord, forgive us.

Leader: For the words which have wounded you, we are truly sorry,

All: In your mercy, Lord, forgive us.

Leader: For the thoughts which have betrayed you, we are truly sorry,

All: In your mercy, Lord, forgive us.

Leader: For the failures which have let you down, we are truly sorry,

All: In your mercy, Lord, forgive us.

Leader: Almighty God, who forgives all who truly repent, have mercy upon us, pardon and deliver us from all our sins, confirm and strengthen us in all goodness, and keep us in life eternal; through Jesus Christ our Lord. Amen.

Leader: Give thanks to the Lord, because he is good.

All: His love goes on forever.

Leader: Sing a new song to the Lord.

All: He has done wonderful things.

Songs of worship for all ages.

Leader: Do you believe and trust in God the Father, who made the world?

All: I believe and trust in him.

Leader: Do you believe and trust in his Son, Jesus Christ, who redeemed mankind?

All: I believe and trust in him.

Leader: Do you believe and trust in his Holy Spirit, who gives life to the people of God?

All: I believe and trust in him.

Leader: This is the faith of the church.

All: This is our faith. We believe and trust in one God, Father, Son and Holy Spirit.

Prayers of thanksgiving led by a group of children, a family, a home group, or an adult.

Short talk for all ages, which introduces the day's teaching theme.

(If children are having teaching in separate age-groups, they leave at this point.)

Songs of worship for adults.

Bible reading.

Prayers of intercession.

Hymn.

Sermon (or, if children and adults are together for the whole service, all age-talk).

Hymn.

Leader: Glory to God in the highest.
All: And peace to his people on earth.
Leader: Go in peace to love and serve the Lord.
All: In the name of Christ, we will.

(Absolution and creed © *The Alternative Service Book*, 1980)

Structured all-age communion

Welcome.

Hymn of praise.

Bible reading.

Songs of worship.

Statement of belief.

Prayers of intercession.

Hymn.

Sermon (or, if children and adults are together for the whole service, all-age talk).

Hymn.

Leader: We are the family of God.
All: We are in the presence of our good Father.
Leader: Let us welcome our brothers and sisters in Christ.

During a pause in the service, adults have an opportunity to greet each other and to introduce themselves to those they do not know. If children have had teaching in separate age-groups, they enter at this point and are welcomed by their families and friends. If desired, refreshments could be served.

The Lord's prayer.

Representatives of children's groups show what they have been making or preparing, or are interviewed about what they have been learning. A member of the congregation explains what the subject of the adults' teaching has been.

Songs of worship and prayers of thanksgiving for all ages, responding to the day's theme.

Call to confession, prayer of repentance, absolution.

Leader: Here is a loaf of bread.
Children: We will remember Jesus.
Leader: Here is a cup of wine.
Children: We will remember Jesus.
Leader: Watch as the bread is broken.
Children: We will remember Jesus.
Leader: Watch as the wine is poured.
Children: We will remember Jesus.
Leader: Now the bread will be eaten.
Children: We will remember Jesus.
Leader: Now the wine will be drunk.
Children: We will remember Jesus.
Leader: Jesus said, 'Do this in memory of me'.
All: We will remember Jesus.

Consecration prayer and administration of communion.

Hymn.

Leader: We have eaten bread to remember Christ.
All: May his praise fill our lives.
Leader: We have drunk wine to remember Christ.
All: May his peace fill our lives.
Leader: Let us spread the good news through all the earth.
All: May his service fill our lives.
Leader: Jesus is with us to the end of the age.
All: May his Spirit fill our lives. Amen.

Unstructured all-age service

Welcome.

Hymn of praise.

Sharing of news for which the congregation can be thankful to God, open first to children, then to all.

Songs and shouts of praise, prayers of thanksgiving, both prepared and spontaneous, and suitable for all ages.

Short talk for all ages, which introduces the day's teaching theme.

(If children have teaching in separate age groups, they leave at this point.)

Songs of worship for adults (if children and adults are together for the whole service, children have a creative or artistic activity as their offering of worship).

Open time for listening to the Holy Spirit, sharing words of prophecy or tongues with their interpretations, psalms or other readings from Scripture, spontaneous outbursts of praise.

Bible reading.

Sermon (or, if children and adults are together for the whole service, all-age talk).

Response to sermon with open prayers of confession and intercession, or private prayer and ministry, or preparation and administration of communion.

Hymn and closing prayer.

SELECT BIBLIOGRAPHY

All-age Worship, Maggie Durran (Angel Press)

All God's Children, General Synod Board of Education (Church House Publishing)

Children Finding Faith, Francis Bridger (Scripture Union)

Children in the Way, General Synod Board of Education (Church House Publishing)

Children in the Worshiping Community, David Ng and Virginia Thomas (John Knox Press, Atlanta USA)

Going to church with Children, Pauline Stewart, Stan Stewart and Richard Green (Joint Board of Christian Education, Melbourne Australia)

Help! There's a Child in my church!, Peter Graystone (Scripture Union)

Leaves on a Tree, Dorothy Jamall (Church House Publishing)

Nurturing Children in Communion, Colin Buchanan (Grove Booklets)

Patterns for Worship, General Synod Liturgical Commission (Church House Publishing)

Pick and Mix, ed. Margaret Dean (Church House Publishing)

Springboard to Worship, Susan Sayers (Kevin Mayhew Ltd)

Taking Children Seriously, Richard Hubbard (Marshall Pickering)

The Dramatised Bible, ed. Michael Perry (Marshall Pickering and the Bible Society)

The Dynamics of Religion, Bruce Read (Darton Longman and Todd) out of print

The Rise and Development of the Sunday School Movement in England, Philip Cliff (National Christian Education Council)

Will our Children have Faith?, John Westerhoff (Dove Communications, Sydney Australia)